"Good news! Non-dual consciousness and radical embodiment are not mutually exclusive. Maybe you, like I, have known this all along; known it in the cells of your own holy body, touched this truth in the depths of silence, live it and teach it and forget and remember it. This collection of luminous essays points us beyond language to the undifferentiated field of being that turns out to be nothing less than Love Itself. Enter."

—**Mirabai Starr**, author of *Wild Mercy*, and
translator of *Dark Night of the Soul*

"In this glorious compendium of thinkers who live and work on the frontiers of the art and science of consciousness, we have a book that opens portals to worlds that astonish while advancing the human mind and spirit. For in these pages, we are met with numinous knowledge and priceless wisdom from those who have 'been there.' Here, too, is the paradox of living in a biodegradable space-time suit and being the universe in miniature. Ultimately, these essays constitute a kind of a text for those who have 'consciously' enrolled in God School! Thus, what you read here both inspires and signals a new and possibly saving agenda for the human species and the Earth we dwell upon."

—**Jean Houston, PhD**, chancellor of
Meridian University, chairman of the
United Palace of Spiritual Arts, researcher
and teacher in human capacities and social
artistry, and author

"*On the Mystery of Being* is a testimony to the courageous and open-minded spirit of inquiry that characterizes the Science and Non-Duality community."

—**Rupert Spira**, teacher of Non-Duality and author of several books, including *The Nature of Consciousness* and *Being Aware of Being Aware*

"Human civilization will only survive if we are able to create communities whose members do not find happiness in excessive material consumption, but in relationships among each other and with the entire community of life. This book of many voices shows beautifully that Maurizio and Zaya have created such a community."

—**Fritjof Capra**, author of *The Web of Life*, and coauthor of *The Systems View of Life*

ON THE
MYSTERY
OF BEING

**Contemporary Insights on the Convergence
of Science and Spirituality**

Edited by
ZAYA and MAURIZIO BENAZZO

REVEAL PRESS
AN IMPRINT OF NEW HARBINGER PUBLICATIONS

Publisher's Note

Distributed in Canada by Raincoast Books

Copyright © 2019 by Science and Nonduality
Non-Duality Press
An imprint of New Harbinger Publications, Inc.
5674 Shattuck Avenue
Oakland, CA 94609
www.newharbinger.com

Cover design by Helena Zingarella

Acquired by Elizabeth Hollis Hansen

Edited by Tony Kendrew

Copy edited by Teja Watson

Library of Congress Cataloging-in-Publication Data on file

Printed in the United States of America

21   20   19

10   9   8   7   6   5   4   3   2   1   First Printing

To all the burning hearts who dare to dream the immensity of life, question the limits of knowledge, and surrender to the mystery of being!

Contents

Foreword

DEEPAK CHOPRA

What is the best, simplest, and most useful thing we can say about our existence? This rich anthology of many voices is essentially asking that question. Whatever the goal of the spiritual path might be, or the objective of science, it must be buried somewhere in existence. Where else could it be? But existence seems to be the ultimate Sphinx, keeping an eternal secret about what is hiding inside—and the secret is so hidden that you might not even guess that there is a secret.

Most of us are brought up to believe that existence is nothing more than a blank canvas. But if that's true, there would be little to say about it. We'd be better off filling in the blank with something meaningful. Seven billion people are born facing an unknown future, so they do the sensible thing; they begin to invent a story about what life means, one person at a time. The experiences they accumulate wind up being part of their personal story. To a creature endowed with free will, it's a great setup. "My story is unique, and everyone else is free to explore their own uniqueness."

Only one glitch spoils this setup, but it's a big one. Using all their intelligence, creativity, family support, social connections, and anything else at their disposal, no one has yet devised a way to rid their story of pain and suffering. Seven billion of us are, in effect, experimenting with the problem of finding happiness, and so far there has been no single discovery—like Thomas Edison's, which lit up the world—to rid our minds and hearts of suffering.

Yet it may be that people are experimenting not with bad ideas or flawed stories, but from the wrong starting point. The stories begin because we assume that existence is a blank canvas. What if it isn't? From the blank canvas perspective, "I am" is an empty statement, and life doesn't get on the road until the sentence is expanded to "I am X." If you replace X with "a white Western male born of a well-to-do family," the chances are your story is going to turn out much better than someone who says, "I am a poor black woman in Senegal in the middle of a drought with six children."

But a few people—by good fortune a sizable group of them have contributed to this book—investigate "I am" without feeling that "X" must follow. What if "I am" is actually the most meaningful thing you can say about yourself? Then you would be looking directly at being, the topic of this anthology. It would be wonderful if being was enough, if existence was not empty, but full of potential, eager to unfold if only we ask it to. In the nondual tradition, which goes back several thousand years, the teaching holds that being is indeed filled with infinite potential. The Vedic rishis who declared "I am That" were pointing not to anything specific, but to a field of indescribable possibilities. These possibilities are not hidden from everyday life. *Homo sapiens*, as a conscious species, constantly takes advantage of fundamental traits that are sourced from existence itself. These traits include creativity, intelligence, will, desire, insight, love, compassion, and self-awareness.

Once you realize that existence is a conscious state, the field of infinite potential is no longer abstract. It exists, in plenitude, here and now. I side with thinkers who say that life can only be lived here and now. Everything else is a dream or spell or illusion concocted by the mind. It testifies to the enormous trauma inflicted by past suffering that the human race would rather exist in a mind-made, dream-spell of illusion than wake up, live in the present moment, and take advantage of our infinite potential.

Here is where the trail divides for nondualists. Like the physician who must offer a correct diagnosis before delivering a cure, nondualists must account for duality (the sickness) before delivering a method for waking up (the cure). That's a tricky business when it comes to the person we know best—ourselves—and far harder when it comes to other people. It has been all too easy to take a short cut and invent a new story—call it religion or spirituality—that neatly catalogues everything as good or bad, helpful or unhelpful for waking up, pleasing or displeasing to God, and so on.

These shortcuts came about out of necessity. "I am That" refers to something indescribable, formless, without substance or qualities, unborn, undying, and beyond language. People wanted something they could see and feel and hold on to. In the Old Testament, Jacob wrestled with an angel. He was lucky; wrestling with duality, entangled in the dream-spell of illusion, is far harder. But if we remain true to "I am," there is no need to wrestle with anything, including oneself.

The flaw in every story, even the most spiritually inspiring ones, is that they always involve a choice. As soon as the mind is faced with either/or, duality has won. It wins by setting the terms of the path that lies ahead, and such a path only leads deeper into duality.

I feel confident that every author in this anthology has reached much the same conclusion. The emergence of monism, nonduality, and panpsychism in our time indicates an advanced stage of getting unstuck from duality. The next step, I believe, is to arrive at a process for awakening that is based on *choiceless awareness*. When you are enmeshed in duality, life is nothing but choices, the countless decisions, big and small, that life demands of us. But each step on the path to waking up reveals how many choices can be done away with. Rid your life of whatever is an illusion, and nothing will remain but what is real.

Some choices can be done away with fairly easily. You can make violence a non-choice, writing it out of your life. You can write out needing to have enemies. You can stop thinking of us-versus-them. But even then, if you drop what is obviously detrimental and adopt something better in its place, a choice is being made. Choiceless awareness can only exist by living in the now. What you do or say or think should have no history or baggage. That's what the now is about. You are not repeating the known, but opening up to the unknown. In a word, you are testing if being here is enough.

If it is, then the next thing you say, think, or do will be right. A big "whoa" crops up when you consider that statement, because at bottom we don't trust the now. We don't trust ourselves to live in it. No matter how many right choices you've made in your life, the risk of making a wrong choice, maybe a very damaging wrong choice, keeps us in a constant state of wary mistrust.

What we are really mistrusting is existence. There has to be a shift of allegiance away from the wary ego-personality, which is always carrying baggage and trying to be guided by the past. Our allegiance needs to return to the source. No other shift carries such importance. The spontaneous fulfillment of desire, the effortless advance of evolution, the inspired answer, the sudden insight, the unexpected rush of joy and love—these things comprise choiceless awareness. We don't need to label them as spiritual or hold them out as the fruits of higher consciousness. Choiceless awareness is how the universe and every cell in your body already gets along.

The fact that existence is by definition consciousness is a fact that can be seen by the utmost rationalist with no claims to spirituality. In a 1931 interview with the *Observer* newspaper in London, the originator of quantum theory, Max Planck, said, "I regard consciousness as fundamental. I regard matter as derivative from consciousness. We cannot get behind consciousness. Everything that we talk about, everything that we regard as existing, postulates consciousness."

If existence is the same as consciousness, and if consciousness is a field of infinite potential, then being here must open a door to that very field.

I don't mean to venture too far into my own personal conclusions about being. The voices in this book offer an eloquent variety of viewpoints, and being is a big subject—the biggest. All I want to say is that everyday life should have an open-door policy. The unknown, which we meet at every moment, is a treasure house, and what it contains cannot be defined or put into words. The rishis who said, "I am That," were also saying, "This is what awaits everyone, once they wake up."

I started by asking what is the best, simplest, and most useful thing we could say about our existence. Here's my answer: "Being here is enough." In the simplicity of that sentence you can hold on to the highest vision of your own life and of our species. "I am" is worthy of investigating every day, and the reward is that consciousness begins to know itself, until there is nothing but the play of consciousness, seeking no other goal but to unfold its own potential.

Acknowledgments

This book would not have been possible without our editor Tony Kendrew's dedication and passion for the subject. A special thank you to Jeanric Meller for helping us carve the introduction to each chapter. Thank you, Helena Zingarella, for creating the beautiful artwork for the cover, which captures so eloquently the essence of SAND. We bow to all the teachers, scientists, and visionaries for their generous support of this book, for their humble and clear presence.

Words cannot express our gratitude to Sheila Klink who has trusted in SAND since the beginning and fearlessly supported us over the years.

We feel grateful to our publisher New Harbinger for initiating this project.

SAND's journey would not have happened without the unconditional support of all the dedicated presenters who have joined us over the years, our fearless team, and all the amazing volunteers, supporters, and attendees who have helped us grow and evolve in time.

We are eternally grateful for the teachings of Sri Nisargadatta Maharaj.

Introduction

Twelve years ago, a beautiful woman attended a workshop in San Francisco. A man tried all he could to get her attention—unsuccessfully. She showed no interest, but at least she took his business card.

A few days later, the man received a phone call from the woman, who said, "I see you make movies about Sri Nisargadatta Maharaj... I love the book *I Am That*. It has been in my hands constantly for two years now."

"Yes," he told her. "Actually, I am going to India in a few weeks to shoot another film about his Indian translators."

To his surprise he heard the woman say, "I am a filmmaker, and I'd love to help."

And that is how Zaya and Maurizio got together and, on one of their first dates, went to India to shoot a film called *Rays of the Absolute,* about the legacy of Sri Nisargadatta Maharaj. In India, one of Nisargadatta's translators told them, "Maharaj used to say: One day scientists will come and understand all this. What I am teaching is not spirituality; it is science."

On our return to the States, we began exploring what Maharaj really meant by this statement, and what modern science has to say about who we are, about the nature of reality and how that connects to what the ancient mystics saw and experienced. We decided to organize an event with the obscure name Science and Nonduality (now referred to as SAND). We didn't expect much from it, other than to gather together a few crazy dreamers like us. To our surprise, three hundred people showed up in a remote conference room in San Rafael, California. Over the years it become apparent that this quest, this longing to bring science and spirituality together, was a collective dream that we share with many.

Both science and spirituality reflect our human urge to know— that perennial itch to make sense of the world and who we are. This quest is an essential part of being human. We probe reality as best we can with our tools of understanding—structures, models, theories, myths, beliefs, teachings—but these tools of understanding also define the limits of our knowledge.

At SAND, we gather to share this almost sensual longing to know the unknowable, to embody that which is beyond any form, to experience the source in its multitude of manifestations, to perceive the infinite through finite cycles. We navigate that space where something else takes over—call it intuition, deep knowing, trust, surrender—a place from which new discoveries in science and realizations in spirituality become possible.

We collectively draw knowledge and wisdom from many spiritual traditions, we learn from the explorations and discoveries of modern science, and we share our understanding and experience of what we learn and realize on this path of awakening.

Our community gathers from all around the globe to explore, learn, and express what it means to be an awakened human being today. We are here not to transcend the world, but to attune to its sacredness in deeper and subtler ways—not to leave what is here and now for some other reality or dimension, but to realize that spirit and matter are not two separate things, but simply ways of seeing an undivided whole. This is nonduality—the philosophical, spiritual, and scientific understanding of the intrinsic oneness of existence.

The essence of modern spirituality is that we humans are full of paradoxes, yet penetrated by mystery. Transcendence and immanence are two sides of the same coin. Enlightenment is intimacy with any experience that arises in this human being. In a nutshell, we are perfectly divine in our imperfect human form.

SAND is a playground where we come together to explore where science and spirituality meet—in the beauty of the questions, in the wonder, facing the unknowable on the edge of the known.

This book is an emergent collection of essays and insights that reflect on the evolution of this collective journey. We invite you to read each piece with an open heart and mind and to notice the invisible thread that weaves them together, remembering that we can never understand, but only surrender to the mystery we call life.

There is no ultimate truth. No teacher, no scientist will give us all the answers. Let us simply bow to the intelligence of our hearts, drop into not knowing, keep our minds open, cherish the questions, and let the answers arise and evolve, all the while celebrating this mystery called life.

Thank you for being here, for reading this book. Welcome home!

PART ONE

Voices of Contemporary Spirituality

When we began our spiritual journey, we searched long and hard for a teacher and a path. We traveled to India, studied sacred texts, and tried many different practices. The beginning of SAND itself was inspired by the desire to bring together all the pointers we had found along our journey and share them with our community.

It is a time-honored truth that there are many different paths, but only one reality. In our interconnected world, spiritual knowledge that may have been kept hidden for centuries is just one click away. In this new paradigm, the roles of teachers and mystics have also shifted.

The spiritual teacher is no longer seen as a perfect being that once attained eternal knowledge and now lives in constant bliss. The new mystics are open, authentic, and human; they speak of "ordinary awakening" and live among us. They are open to dialogue with teachers from other traditions, and even with scientists.

They do not lead us toward a special state, nor do they speak of transcending our human form. They invite us not to take anything for granted, but to explore, question, and carefully investigate everything through our own direct experience.

Today's spiritual teachers point to the intelligence of our hearts and spark a love affair with truth and wonder. They meet us where we are, in our very struggle, and invite us to tend to our human experience while remembering our divine nature. They direct us to discover each and every moment as the ultimate teacher and remind us that we are never apart from the mystery, from the truth of existence, from consciousness, from God.

In the following pages you will meet some of these new teachers, the human beings that we have met personally and who have touched our hearts, people like you and us sharing their experience, their love for the mystery, and their humanity.

May their words shine light on our path, may they open our hearts.

—Maurizio and Zaya

Love and Wonder

ADYASHANTI

You're probably reading this book because of a sense of love—a great love of questions and wonder. We have an instinct within us to understand ourselves, and the world we live in, in a very deep way.

Spirituality is a wonderment with the experience of being—of existence, in whatever way you want to approach it. Spirituality is an exploration of the most fundamental, existential questions of being: Who am I? What is the world? Where did this all come from?

These are the same questions that people from many different pursuits outside of spirituality are exploring—scientists of all sorts, mathematicians, physicists. We share a love for similar questions. These questions seem to be rooted in the structure of consciousness, through this common wonderment.

We also have a desire to experience what we know, or what we think we know. We long to connect the wonderment of the intellect and the wonderment of experience—not to be satisfied with only one part of that equation. We're always exploring and experiencing these deep mysteries that we come upon.

Spirituality and science can seem so divergent, but in the fundamental and deep questions they ask, they come together.

Ordinary Awakening

GANGAJI

In religious and spiritual movements, we often unnecessarily and tragically separate truth into an enclave of transcendence. I would never deny the transcendent qualities of self-realization, but until we recognize that the truth is alive in each of us—just as we are, in our own particular and unique ways, in our own particular circumstances and communities—we have realized only partial truth.

I had always imagined that realizing the truth would mean that the personality would disappear, or perhaps this form would dissipate into holy vapor. But actually, and importantly, it was very ordinary—and most intimate. This form actually became more ordinary than ever. My opinions still arose, thoughts still arose, emotions still arose, but there was no more mistaking these for reality.

I had heard the teaching that the world of form is illusion, and I imagined that the realization of a formless nonduality would involve some sort of disappearance. Quite the contrary—it has been an endless delight to find that this limitless presence of conscious life is present regardless of formation. It is all. It is the source of and the very substance of every thought formation, every emotion, every circumstance, every creature.

In this moment, you are eternal truth. Everything that you imagine yourself to be arises in that truth, exists in that truth, and disappears back into that truth. Truth is the essential nature of consciousness, and consciousness is the source of individual awareness. Truth is the essence of life. Truth is who you are.

The byproducts of this realization can be beautiful and exalted and earth-shattering, yet at the same time unspeakably ordinary, mundane, and human. The truth is that your life, precisely as it is, has the capacity to be conscious of itself as *life itself*. In this recognition, we can live the rest of our moments, our days, our decades, effortlessly conscious of conscious life. This is the true adventure of living. This is the recognition of conscious, ever-present being.

Can you live with all the ups and downs of the experience of being human, and still be conscious of, and nurtured by, the truth of who you are? *Yes!* Awakening to this truth is not just for the sages of the past—it is for you too. This is a time of ordinary awakening. If you can cross the line into conscious self-recognition, then everything that arises in your awareness does so only to deepen that conscious self-recognition. The rest of your lifetime can be lived in that recognition and in the celebration and the sharing of that.

Once an awakening has occurred in the boundless, unconditional freedom of your true nature, is there then a responsibility to live in a certain way in the world?

To this I would also answer yes! When you are called home, when you are somehow struck by the absolutely mysterious and irrevocable desire to know the truth of who you are, then you must be willing to put aside every story of separation. Every story of separation is a story of war.

Human beings have been making war for all time. Culture is a reflection of the individual mind, as the individual mind is a reflection of the cultural mind. If you investigate the terrible events that are happening all over the world, it's not difficult to see that the human-caused events begin as reactions to anger and fear, to deep grief and despair. In seeing this, it becomes apparent that these external events are the result of the same dynamics happening within us. If we can recognize in our individual lives how we resist surrender, how we resist our vulnerability, how we grapple daily for power or control, then we can recognize the tendency toward war within ourselves—the tendencies of totalitarianism, hate, revenge, and dominance—and we can directly recognize the suffering that those tendencies continue to deliver.

If we are willing to take responsibility for our own depth of awakening, for our own peace—if we can end the war on just this one spot of Mother Earth (you!)—then we are actually available to effect bigger change. Then at least this one place is at peace, is free. Whenever any of us chooses peace within our own mind and heart, an enormous force of energy and attention is freed. To be peace is to offer peace. Only then will we see what can truly arise on this earth.

For most of us, certainly for those who have the leisure to read these words, we aren't in the worst of situations. In this moment we don't need to run from bombs or bullets, from imminent rape or starvation. We have shelter for the night—although we all must know that this privilege could change within a heartbeat, at any place or time, whether from political upheaval or natural disaster. But right now, many of us in communities all over the world have the good luck of being able to truly investigate our responsibility as human beings on our planet at this time. Our privilege provides the possibility of self-reflection, and the opportunity to earnestly inquire into what is true. Who are we, really?

You are not alone in this awakening. There are people all over the world at this very moment with the same commitment. Without denying the waves of terror and suffering on our planet, we can recognize that right now there is a great wave of support for awakening, for the whole human race to actually shift its perspective of war, terror, and hatred to one of openness and acceptance. Each one of us is essential.

When I use the word "responsibility," I am not talking about responsibility as a whip, a burden, or even a duty. I am inviting you to take responsibility for the truth of who you are, in this precious body, in this precious human incarnation, for this precious time on Mother Earth.

Many people I speak with across the globe seem so beaten down and bound by their own internal self-abuse that inner freedom eludes them. Yet the way out is quite simple, if often supremely challenging. It means saying "no" to the totalitarian voice in our heads and "yes" to the possibility of inner equanimity. "Yes" to inclusion. I am suggesting that you simply open your mind and allow your life to be used by the force that is alive in your heart.

Closer to Heaven, Closer to the Mud

JEFF FOSTER

I recall the moment my dear father passed from this world. One final exhale, and he fell into infinite silence and deep rest. I was filled with an ancient sadness, not just my own sadness but the sadness of all sons saying good-bye to their fathers throughout history. I was vast, filled with the hearts of all who have ever mourned, and yet I was minuscule, dwarfed by a sublime mystery that I had no hope of comprehending. Good-bye, dear father. Rest well.

And yet in the very same moment, I felt a great joy—the joy of being alive to witness such a moment. Such sacredness in this pain, such holiness in this most profound loss! I was broken, yet I was whole. In the depths of the mess of the moment, in this dark under-world of death, there was such ferocious light, such blinding love. When we are awake and no longer numb, we can open our hearts to all these paradoxes, and let go of ever resolving them. We enter life and are entered in return. We know less and we feel more. We break more deeply and more light breaks through. We are more transpar-ent, more supple. We are beginners again, newcomers in the Garden of Eden, eyes wide open and full of wonder.

I sense that the old spirituality is crumbling. The sad patriarchal spirituality that suppressed the feminine, shamed the body—its feel-ings and its mortality—frowned upon our sexuality and our long-ings, and tried to numb our deepest questions and urges to protect the image of "the calm, peaceful one," or worse, "the invulnerable, untouchable one," or even worse, "the pain-free superhuman." A spirituality that wanted to eradicate our anger, and tried to liberate us from our sadness, fear, and doubts, so we could be pure and enlightened and "free."

Something new is emerging now: a spirituality that actually *embraces* our humanity in all its mess and its longings, its ecstasy and its bliss, its intense pleasure and its outrageous pain. A spirituality that does not seek to eradicate our weirdness and our wildness, our humor and our originality and our broken, tender hearts...but renders it all so damn holy, and finds freedom in the midst of it. A spirituality in which there are no "experts," no gurus in the old sense, no special states to attain, no "finish lines." Just vulnerable human beings, falling in love with "what is," drenching our ordinary moments with curiosity.

Spirit is not separate from flesh. The ocean is undivided from her myriad waves. The sky is in love with the sloppiest mud. The artist adores and needs his dark colors as much as his light ones, and the great canvas holds it all. Spiritual enlightenment is nothing if it is not warm and wild and sticky and gooey and human; if it does not allow and honor the full range of deep human feeling, from despair to ecstasy, from the most brilliant clarity to the most profound confusion. Nonduality is nothing if it is not a tantric love affair with this glorious, artistic mess of duality. Awareness is nothing if it is not radically in love with every form—every thought, sensation, sound, and smell, every wave of anger, fear, and sorrow—that arises and falls on its astonishing canvas.

We are not simply "Pure Awareness"—no, we are sex and dirt and longing too. We are blood and guts and passion. We are wildness and we are fire. We are gods, and we are so very fragile—heartbroken gods, gods who ache, imperfect gods. We are invulnerable, untouchable, indestructible, and yet we can sometimes feel the world's pain as our own. We live so close to life, so close to death, so close to tears, so close to joy, in every single moment. Close to the heavens, close to the mud, close to insanity, close to the breath. We bleed sometimes. We feel exhausted sometimes. Sometimes we just need a brother or sister to hold us. Sometimes we tire of being "the spiritual one," "the one who knows," "the expert," "the enlightened one," "the good and compassionate one."

Sometimes we just need to fall to our knees in humility and ask the universe for support and guidance. Sometimes we just need to weep until our tear ducts run dry. Sometimes we need to curse and rage at the sky and forget what it means to be "spiritual." Sometimes, that's how healing happens. When we give up trying and give ourselves permission to break open and make a mess and fall, and we let the ground hold us, and we remember, *It's all okay, it's all so fucking okay.* We are full of paradoxes. Penetrated by mystery.

The age of gurus and disciples may be over. The age of experts and their clever mind-made answers may be coming to an end. Let the birdsong be the guru now, the morning traffic, the touch of a friend, the tingle in the belly, your four-year-old niece giggling at pigeons and melted ice cream, your sweet father taking his final breath in the last light of the evening. Saying good-bye to a friend after a sweet day of conversation and comfortable silence, not knowing when—or if—you will meet again. A sorrow, a yearning, a joy or an emptiness that just longs to be *felt.* The dawn and the sunrise. The ocean and the light. *Life, life, life.* Let the holy books dissolve into a fresh new moment. Let us bow to the ordinary now, prostrate ourselves before it.

Here. Here. Be a disciple of this: the unspeakable feeling of the breath rising and falling. The heart pounding in the chest. An airplane roaring in the distance. The magical weight of the physical body as gravity pulls it down toward the earth's core. The aliveness in the toes, the hands, the throat, the sexual organs. The pressure in the head, the yearning and the expectancy of the dear heart, and this wonderful sense of being alive, prior to words, prior to all the teachings of the world.

There are no experts, here where you are. There is only a single living question, the question that is meditation itself—unanswerable, yet complete and beautiful in its absolute unresolvability: *What is life?*

ON THE MYSTERY OF BEING

The Magic of Shared Awareness

SALLY KEMPTON

A doe and two fawns often visit my back garden. They settle in under the oaks, keeping a close eye on my window. If I'm on the porch, they will engage with me in long moments of mutual eye-gazing. It often feels as if they are beaming a kind of affectionate curiosity in my direction. At moments, it can seem as if presence in the deer is gazing at presence in me.

One of the sweetest ways I know of to recognize nondual presence is to gaze into the eyes of another being. The first spiritual group I worked with, in the 1970s, practiced left-eye gazing. If you've done that practice, you know how psychedelic it can be. You look at someone's face, and watch it morph and shift. Young faces take on sage-like qualities of wisdom, then become fierce or opaque. They can shift gender, or age fifty years in a moment. Sometimes you see ten or twenty different faces on the same person. Our group got fascinated with these phenomena for a while, but it soon became clear that something deeper, something much more interesting, was going on.

Over time, I discovered that if two people could let go of their various fears and agendas, they would both enter a space of insight, love, and connectedness that was profound and dynamic. The gaze of the other person catalyzed a connection to awareness itself. When we talked about our experience later, we'd often remark that there seemed to be no such thing as "my awareness" and "your awareness." There was only one awareness, and it was shared. When you meditate with another person, with eyes open, and the intention to allow shared awareness to reveal itself, something greater than the two of you emerges. Awareness shared is awareness squared, awareness to the nth power. In those moments, there is no other.

I believe that human intimacy is, at its core, an experiment in recognizing shared awareness in the midst of apparent difference. Think about your moments of deep intimacy. Didn't they include a feeling of entering together into the subtle and tender field of "knowing," a sense of being in touch with a shared recognition of your shared conscious depths?

Some schools of nondual wisdom say that individual humans are vehicles through which pure awareness—the transpersonal intelligence that underpins life—can experience itself. In this sense, the mind of a human being is an emergent activity of the great mind, of cosmic consciousness itself. When we sit together and focus toward awareness, the thoughts and impressions that define us as egoic selves begin to dissolve. It becomes more possible to feel the presence of the greater field that encloses us all.

Normally, when I'm with another person, their thought stream and my thought stream negotiate, each of us inwardly wondering, *Am I seen? Am I okay in this relationship? Will I get hurt? Is this person my kind of person?*

In meditative intimacy, two people can discover that when they both inhabit aware presence, they create doorways into truth and awareness that can take them far beyond the ordinary level of human communication. Sharing presence in this way is naturally therapeutic, because it lets you hold your own or someone else's suffering in a field of acceptance. It is inherently creative, because it allows ideas and solutions to surface out of the shared field.

More than that, it is a doorway into the infinite.

Traditionally, if you practiced sharing awareness with another person, it was with a guru or teacher, and the transmission of consciousness only went one way. Eye-to-eye transmission of shakti has always been a technique by which a teacher transmits grace and inner states of awareness to a student. If you were the student, you tried to take in the high or enlightened or loving state of the teacher, and if you were the teacher you intended to pass on your state to the student.

Yet peer-to peer transmission is the true heart of spiritual community. Once we realize that each of us can connect soul to soul, awareness to awareness, it becomes natural to be able to awaken each other through our gaze. Of course, the more clarity and love each of us has cultivated, the more powerful the transmission that we can offer another. But because awareness is ever-present, it is not so hard to develop the skill of opening to that space with someone else. Once you've glimpsed it, once you've felt it, there is a neurological memory of it inside your system, and then it's a matter of coming back to it again and again until you develop a real sense of what it feels like to be in presence, both alone and with someone else.

A Practice for Shared Awareness

It's helpful to cultivate shared awareness with an informal protocol. I like to do it by combining an inner body awareness (dropping into my heart-center) with an awareness of three things: the heart-space in my partner, the space behind my body at the level of the heart, and the space behind the other person's heart.

As in any meditation, you notice and let go of thoughts or emotions or fears as they arise. As you develop the sense of a spatial connection that is independent of your thoughts about each other, you become able to inhabit a sense of presence that encloses and includes both of you. You can rest in your own awareness and simultaneously connect with the other person, not trying to impose any agenda on the experience or on the person you're working with.

At that point, it becomes possible not only to sit in shared spacious presence together, but also to access wisdom together. The relationship that forms in those moments is not simply empathic. You become embodiments of sacred presence for each other, in which truths can be spoken, even tough ones, in which enormous vulnerability can be accessed and healed. This happens because the consciousness-space is intrinsically healing and transformative.

To practice in this shared space of consciousness is to realize and know that human intimacy is a true portal into wholeness—a doorway into the divine.

The Essence of the Mind

RUPERT SPIRA

All knowledge and experience is known in the mind, by the mind. Therefore, in order to know what anything truly is, it is first necessary to know the nature of the mind through which it is known. We cannot be sure that the mind's knowledge of the universe is anything more than a reflection of its own limitations. Therefore, there can be no higher knowledge, nor any higher endeavor, than to know the nature of the mind.

What is it that can investigate or know the nature of the mind? The mind is that through which all things are known, and therefore the mind can only be investigated by itself. The name that the mind gives itself is "I," "myself." Therefore, the mind's investigation into itself is the investigation into who or what I essentially am. "What is the essential nature of the mind?" and "Who or what am I?" are, therefore, two ways of formulating the same question, the answer to which is the absolute knowledge upon which all other relative knowledge must be founded.

Who or what am I? I am seeing these words, I am knowing my current thoughts, I am aware of my feelings. "I," the essence of the mind, accompanies all experience, irrespective of its content. "I" could be likened to a golden thread that runs through a beaded necklace. When we look at the necklace we cannot see the thread, but without the thread there would be no necklace. "I," the golden thread that runs throughout all experience, cannot be known or seen as an object of experience, and yet without it there would be no experience. If we remove one, ten, or all of the beads from the necklace, it is still a necklace. If we remove all thoughts and perceptions from experience, we are still our self. Only that which remains when all the objects of experience have been removed qualifies as "I" or the essence of the mind.

"I" is the illuminating or knowing factor in all knowledge and experience, and as all there is to experience is the knowing of it, "I," the essence of the mind or pure consciousness, is all that is ever truly known. Just as, relatively speaking, the sun's light renders the world visible, so "I" renders experience knowable. It's not a physical light but a knowing light, a knowing presence that illuminates, knows, or is aware of all experience. It renders all experience knowable but is not itself an experience. It is the essential ingredient in all experience but cannot itself be found as an object of experience.

The mind that tries to find its own essence is like a character in a movie in search of the screen. The screen never appears as an object in the movie, and for this reason the character can never find the screen in her world. And yet, at the same time, all she ever experiences is the screen. Likewise, the essence of the mind never appears as an object in the mind, and yet all the mind ever experiences is itself. It is the light of pure knowing or consciousness upon which the drama of experience plays, with which it is known and ultimately out of which it is made, and yet it is not itself an experience.

We are too close to our self to know our self in subject/object relationship, just as the sun is too close to itself to be able to turn around and shine on itself or illuminate itself. The sun illuminates every other planet by shining the rays of its light toward that planet, but it cannot shine the rays of its light on itself. Nor does it need to; it illuminates itself just by being itself. Likewise, all the objects of experience are known or illuminated by the mind, but the mind is too close to itself to be able to direct its knowing or its attention toward its own essence. Nor does it need to; it is already standing as itself. It knows itself simply by being itself.

Therefore, the highest knowledge is simply to know oneself as one essentially is, before our essential self—pure mind or original mind—has been colored or conditioned by experience. This is the only knowledge that does not take place in subject/object relationship, and is thus absolute knowledge, not relative to the condition of the finite mind. It is pure knowing or consciousness, not yet colored by experience.

The "I" or pure mind that is present at the heart of all experience is always in the same condition. Just as the screen is always the same, irrespective of the content of the movie, so the "I" that is present now, knowing or aware of our current experience, is the same "I" that was present knowing whatever we experienced yesterday, last year, or ten years ago. Nothing ever happens to "I," the screen of awareness upon which the drama of experience plays. No experience adds anything to it or removes anything from it. It never evolves or ages; it is never tarnished or hurt by experience; it is never moved or changed. The characters in the movie may grow old and sick and die, but nothing ever happens to their reality, relatively speaking—the screen.

Thoughts may be agitated, feelings disturbed, sensations painful, and perceptions unpleasant, but the "I" with which all experience is known, in which all experience appears, and, ultimately, out of which all experience is made doesn't itself share any of the limited qualities of experience. It is, as such, unlimited or infinite. The objects of experience appear and disappear, but "I," the essence of the mind, remains ever-present and is, as such, eternal. "I" is never disturbed by experience, and thus its nature is peace. "I" doesn't stand to gain or lose anything from experience—it is inherently complete, whole, fulfilled, perfect—and thus its nature is happiness.

Just as all the limited images that appear in a movie are made of the unlimited screen, relatively speaking, so all relative knowledge and experience is made out of eternal, infinite consciousness. The essence of the finite mind is infinite consciousness, and all the mind's knowledge is a refraction of that infinite consciousness. For this reason, science as it is currently practiced will never know the nature of reality. To know the nature of reality, it is first necessary to know the nature of the mind through which reality is known.

To know oneself as one essentially is is the source of the peace and happiness for which all people long, and is the foundation upon which all other knowledge must be built. Thus, the highest science is the science of consciousness. Unless and until the nature of consciousness is understood, scientists will never know the nature of the universe.

Faces of the Infinite in Everyday Life

DOROTHY HUNT

The face before you were born is looking at its self each moment.

The Face of Beauty: Oneness Touching the Senses

I am sitting in my home and a strong afternoon wind has picked up. The leaves on ancient oaks are dancing wildly as moss-covered boulders sit totally unmoved. Lizards continue their push-ups, unfazed. A whirring hummingbird flies by, revealing its red throat and iridescent body. Hillside vineyards are splashed with green, distant ridges washed with muted grays and lavender. A thin layer of clouds renders the sky a pale blue.

In this moment, there is a sense of the vast beauty and wholeness of being, a single reality that includes everything. The colors, life's movements and stillness, the sound of the wind all seem imbued with warmth, aliveness, and intimacy. This intimacy is beyond ideas of subject and object, an intimacy that does not simply "witness," "transcend," or "be with" the moment, but is actually one with life as it is. Here, infinite oneness touches the senses, and the experience is beauty and awe.

The Face of Love: The Infinite Heart We Share

My two youngest grandsons are visiting me. They like to sit close and lean into my body. At the end of this day, the eight-year-old races up from his downstairs bedroom in his pajamas, tightly clutching his stuffed "mama lion," to give me a good-night hug and kiss. We warmly embrace, and both of us feel the current of love that connects us. He tells me that I am welcome to come down anytime if I want more "snuggles."

When the infinite moves in the heart, we experience love, compassion, intimacy, oneness, and gratitude. These are qualities that move spontaneously when we are not separating ourselves from the truth of our being or from the moment. In the infinite heart, we experience love seeing itself.

An open heart is open to suffering as well as joy. Life includes fear, injustice, despair, anger, grief, and death of the form. Yet the true heart does not close. It moves with compassion in response to suffering; it is frequently suffering that leads to the desire to know if something lies beyond.

The Face of Truth: The Mystery Present Here and Now

Totally at one with *every* experience in our daily life is a silent presence awake to the moment. No one owns it, no one creates it, no one can destroy it. It is wordless, yet aware of words; formless, yet one with form. It makes no judgments, holds no opinions, claims no identity, and has no name, though it does not reject any names that thought may give it. Some of those names include True Nature, the Self, Nondual Awareness, the Heart of Awareness, Buddha Nature, the Divine.

Yet words will never capture or define this truth. Writing, speaking, and pointing arise, yet our essential nature is empty of definition, concepts, conditions, or limitations. It is nothing our mind can "know" as an object. It is the knowing itself. It is what we are.

As infinite presence reveals itself through the mind, we experience moments of clarity, wisdom, and insight that do not arise from what is learned, but from our essential nature. Whoever or whatever is in front of us, or within us, is a manifestation of the self that we are—sometimes moving through veils of conditioning that limit our view, but ultimately arising from the heart of awareness that is our true nature.

In Ramana Maharshi's words:

> *The Self is only one. If limited it is the ego,*
> *If unlimited, it is Infinite, and is the Reality.*[1]

The Face of Freedom: No Separate "One"

There simply is no separate "someone" who awakens. What we imagined was a person with a birthdate and future death date is actually transparent in the eyes of deep truth. We are spirit, infinite potential, free beyond birth or death. As the formless takes endless forms moment to moment, experiences simply happen.

Any authentic awakening always carries a shift of identity. But this does not mean taking on a new identity; it means seeing the unreality of our constructed identities. In the movement of life's causes and conditions, the awareness that illuminates appearances is not threatened by any experiences the body-mind may be having; yet it is not separate from them either. There is freedom to *be*, to have the experiences that arise spontaneously. Freedom then moves to unwind illusions and invite our innocent misunderstandings back home to the wholeness of being.

The Face of Wholeness: An Ocean of Awareness

We are living, breathing, eating, sleeping, doubting, crying, laughing, loving in an ocean of awareness and beingness that is life itself. This ocean is totally still and silent in its depths, yet teeming with life, fluidity, and impermanence on its surface. Presence is not

---

1   Ramana Maharshi, Talks with Sri Ramana Maharshi (Tiruvannamalai, Tamil Nadu, India: T. N. Venkataraman, Sri Ramanasramam, 1984), 130.

personal; time does not take us to the timeless; a separate self does not produce love or truth; we can only be awake now.

From undivided wholeness, the true "eye" within sees unity and differences simultaneously. What is awake is already present, at peace, and loving you inside your own heart—closer than a thought or a breath.

Extraordinary Within the Ordinary

Later in the evening, the little ones are sleeping. As I sit sipping tea, I am reminded how life shows its extraordinary truth in the simplest, most ordinary moments of our lives. A hummingbird, a hug, the milk that just spilled, laughter bursting forth, the pattern of light on the wall, the warmth of evening tea, the tenderness of our compassionate heart in the face of pain, the sound of wind moving through the trees, or breathing a gentle breath—all are expressions being sung by spirit, by silence, by a love that is one, a formless mystery that birthed itself as form to see, experience, and love its self.

The Wonder of Unknowing

MAURO BERGONZI

We usually describe the world in terms of trees, mountains, rivers, clouds, cars, houses, people, and so on. But a chemist might say, "No, this is not how things truly are! The world is basically composed of molecules that are ceaselessly combining one with another at random."

However, a physicist might reply, "Not at all! Reality is actually made up of intermingling fields of energy-matter in which the dance of waves-particles takes place ceaselessly."

Who is right? Who is wrong?

These are clearly mere conceptual descriptions that can only supply a relative view of reality. We do not actually live in "reality," but rather in a description of it. It is like a bubble of concepts and words all around us, which in time builds up a fictitious view of ourselves and the world.

Even nondualism (as with any other -ism, without exception) is just a conceptual description of reality, which hopelessly tries to point to the unknowable "whatever it is." And insofar as it becomes an ideology that relies on words and thoughts, it is unable to enjoy the taste of being.

We live in concepts without realizing it. We blindly believe that reality is just as our thought represents it. Science gives us an "objective" description of the material world that, to some extent, can be very useful for the improvement of humankind, however relative and incomplete it is. Nonduality—as far as it relies on words and thoughts—is just another conceptual description of reality, though its understanding of non-separation can dispel a huge amount of suffering in one's life. Neither of these conceptual descriptions is more or less right, and both are useful. But as long as we rely only on them, we remain trapped in the net of concepts.

Just as the fisherman's net can catch only fish, but not the water that passes through it and supports it, so the thinking mind can grasp only concepts, but not the awareness that perceives it as an object. The "water of awareness" can never be detected by the net of the thinking mind.

Indeed, awareness is a paradoxical mystery. On the one hand, its evidence is undeniable, for the very reason that we are aware of objects. On the other hand, it is unknowable—just as the existence of the eye is undeniable for the very reason that we can see objects, though the eye always remains invisible, outside the picture.

However, even "awareness" is just a concept: Through it, we are ultimately confronted with the unknown "bottom line" of any human knowledge. No understanding whatsoever can touch the unknowable source of everything.

What if *any idea* about who I am, including even the idea of "consciousness," totally collapses? What if *any idea* about reality, including even the idea of "nonduality," totally collapses? What if *even these very words you are reading now* lose any meaning whatsoever and fall away? What remains when every attempt to understand or to know reality reveals its utter futility?

Then, out of frustration, the thinking mind cannot help saying "I don't know" and finally quits. But when that "I don't know" plunges from the head into the heart, the philosopher dies and the mystic is born. It is not a process in time. It is a singularity where all the known collapses and disappears. It is a timeless explosion of pure wonder and awe that blows everything else away. And what remains is a wild, free, spontaneous, and utterly unknowable aliveness, within the glowing darkness of the mystery that we ultimately are.

PART TWO

The Rebirth of Metaphysics

Metaphysics is the branch of philosophy that deals with first principles—being, knowing, and identity. It seeks to understand what doesn't change, what was never born and will never die, what remains as the background of all human experience. When we started SAND, that deep longing to understand the nature of reality and who we are was the driving force behind the absurd endeavor to bring scientists and spiritual teachers together for a dialogue. As you can imagine, the dialogue proved challenging—and deeply fulfilling.

This section offers a taste of some of the challenges of such an ambitious dream, which addresses not only what is possible to know, but also how we know it. On the one hand, scientists probe reality by observation and experiment, removing any space for subjectivity. On the other hand, those on the spiritual path use contemplation and their own direct experience as instruments for exploration. In both approaches, these tools of understanding define the limits our knowledge. Is it possible to go beyond the limits of our tools? What would that take?

In the following articles, some of these challenges, and attempts to move beyond them, are addressed. We explore the space where a different kind of knowledge—call it "intuition" or "luminous knowing"—takes over, allowing new discoveries in science and new realizations in spirituality.

What if science and spirituality, while responding to our collective aspiration to grow as a species in a world filled with mystery and wonder, no longer needed to carry the burden of having all the answers? What if the dialogue between science and spirituality was forever open-ended, rather than needing to arrive at a foundational agreement or understanding? What if, while we probe deeper into reality and who we are, we realize that the knowledge we gather is just a stepping stone, and never the arrival at a final destination? And what if we humans can't help but continue to ponder and ask beautiful questions, and organize events where scientists and spiritual teachers share the beauty of the questions and the silence of the mysteries we will never understand?

—Maurizio and Zaya

Nondual vs. Scientific Views of Reality

A. H. ALMAAS

This whole SAND project is about bringing science and nonduality together. For nonduality and science to meet, to dialogue, we need to understand where each of them is coming from. What is the view of nonduality and how does it regard the scientific perspective? And how does the world of science view mystical traditions and nondual experience? We need to have that understanding for there to be a true meeting, instead of just talking about it. The two must touch each other, so that there is a mutual benefit.

Nisargadatta Maharaj said, "Consciousness is the greatest painter. The whole world is a picture." Everything is a picture that consciousness paints. Everything—what you consider you, I, the whole world, the universe, the stars, atoms—all of these are nothing but consciousness and the way consciousness manifests itself. They don't really exist the way that people take them to.

One of the basic things that nonduality says is that the world as known conventionally, which science has been studying—whether from a classical perspective or a quantum perspective—is really all an illusion. There are no microtubules, there are no brains. If you look at all the theories of consciousness, the brain is very important, but from the perspective of consciousness the brain is nothing but consciousness manifesting something that somebody calls a brain. Nisargadatta Maharaj did not think that his experience had been interpreted by his brain. He thought his brain had been interpreted by him, by his consciousness.

In other words, consciousness, or what is called "being" or "true nature" or "Buddha nature," is so fundamental that the usual view that there are people who have individual experiences—and some of those people are scientists who study those experiences and try to understand the basis of matter—is an illusionary way of experiencing reality. And going deeper into the states of matter, into atoms, particles, quarks, strings...from the perspective of a nondualist, it doesn't matter. The idea is to recognize that you are consciousness, and everything is consciousness—and that is the freedom. And this experience of the realization of nonduality has been the same for thousands of years, regardless of the scientific point of view, which keeps changing. In a hundred years, science might be completely different.

From the perspective of a nondualist, the average individual is deluded. In the classic double-slit experiment, for example, whether there is an electron or a wave going through the two slits is irrelevant. From the perspective of a nondualist, there is no electron and no wave. There is nothing that moves that way. Everything is created every instant.

The neuroscientist says we don't know what we perceive; the brain interprets the input from our senses, and that input then creates a picture and we see the world. From the perspective of nonduality there is no input that is going into the brain; that is a story you are telling yourself. The arising of light, of sound, the movement of sound, the brain cell—all of those are created as one unified picture, and that picture is like a movie screen. It keeps moving one frame at a time. The movement of the frame makes it appear as if there is an electron that appears and moves, and we have a theory that the brain interprets that. But the brain itself is seen from the perspective of nonduality as nothing but a manifestation. Just like the whole body, the whole universe is a manifestation of the same consciousness. We are not awake, we are not free, we are not liberated, if we do not recognize that we are this pure awareness, this pure truth. That is the view of nonduality.

I am not saying I'm buying that. I'm saying, that is what nondualists say. I know the experience. I live nonduality; I've lived it for twenty years or so. Before that I lived a few decades in duality. The experience of nonduality makes everything from the perspective of duality delusional, even though people in the dualistic world think that science is improving their understanding of the physical world. Maybe it is. But from the perspective of the nondualist it is irrelevant.

The realization of Nisargadatta Maharaj, and before him of Ramana Maharshi, and a thousand years ago of somebody else, is always that nonduality is forever creating the same universe, regardless of how we understand it. The world is an illusion. It is not how the average person takes it to be, nor how scientists take it to be, whether the scientist is a classical scientist, a quantum physicist, or a neuroscientist. Those are just different stories to explain things from a delusional perspective, the perspective that there are separate brains and each one is having some kind of interpretation of experience.

So we need to understand that nondualists don't care. The real nondualists don't care how science is going. SAND's founders are courageous to say let's bring nonduality and science together, because nondualists say science—whether it's from the time of Euclid and Democritus, or Leibniz and Newton, or Einstein and Plank, or now—continues the same. Everything is a manifestation of consciousness, and to believe it one way or another is just changing the story. It's all an error. There are no individual people who are having individual experiences.

So, that's the first view. Now I want to clarify what scientists say.

We know that even Nisargadatta Maharaj, who says everything is arising in consciousness—even that he is the source of awareness and consciousness—he himself had to go to the toilet and he had to wipe his ass. Regardless how realized the nondualist, when they see a street full of cars, they make sure their body does not cross in front of one.

Physical reality is still with us and its laws are still operative, regardless how much we think of it as a delusion. Delusion or illusion doesn't mean that the physical world doesn't have its own truth. Even the pure nondual master still has to deal with physical matter. They still have to deal with illness.

There's something about the physical world that defies the insights of nonduality and says, "Regardless how much you think I'm a delusion, you'd better be careful." Don't assume the delusion means you need not consider the physical world in the way materialists think of it, the way positivists think of it, the way scientists think of it.

The world of a scientist is not the world of nonduality. The world of the scientist is the physical world. In the classical physical world with billiard ball laws, when cars hit each other, they crash. Quantum physicists would say, "Well, there is no such thing as a crash until you perceive a crash." You can look at it classically or you can look at it quantum-mechanically. If this physical world, this regular, ordinary world, is illusionary, why does this physical world have an order to it even if we're not aware that it is all consciousness? From the perspective of normal people, the world has order and the order can be understood scientifically.

When most scientists hear that everything is consciousness, all is delusion, they think this is just mystical talk. It is superstition. Science became scientific by divorcing itself from the church, from religion. It liberated itself by not taking the religious point of view as the description of reality. *No, we'll do experiments. We'll have to have theories, hypotheses, and we'll have to test them with experiments, which will have to be verified and repeated.* When you tell scientists that everything is consciousness, everything is God, the scientists say, "Wait a minute. We became scientists by pushing that away and now you want to tell us we are wrong, we are all deluded? Look at what we've done. If we're deluded, how could we have done all that?" Most scientists don't believe it. They think those people are naive and superstitious.

Scientists continue to explore things, and now they are trying to understand consciousness—not from the perspective that everything is consciousness, but from the fact that there are living beings who have the capacity to have experiences, to be conscious. They have made great strides, trying to understand where consciousness comes from. Maybe it has to do with deep space-time, as Penrose says, or microtubules or quantum gravity. Quantum theory brings the whole world into question, but they're not saying that it is all consciousness. They believe in particles, in electrons. Nisargadatta Maharaj says, No! There are no electrons. An electron is just the appearance of consciousness. From the perspective of the nondualist, the double-slit experiment is just like any other delusion. But for the scientist, it is a real thing.

We need to think a little more carefully before we say it's a delusion or illusion.

The proposal I have, which comes from my direct experience, is that the nondual way of experiencing is one way of experiencing reality. Obviously, it's a valid way of experiencing reality. The scientific point of view, which makes precise the ordinary dualistic point of view, is also a way of experiencing reality that is just as valid.

Why do we have to think that one of them is right and the other is wrong? Why can't both be correct—that the world can be experienced in two distinct ways? Each has its own validity, truth, and usefulness, and human beings live in both worlds simultaneously all the time. Maybe they will meet. I am not saying they are different realities, I'm saying it's the same reality experienced in different ways. One way is the nondualist way, which has developed many teachings. The other way is the ordinary way that has developed science.

I do not live in either one of them. I don't live a nondual reality and I don't live a dualistic reality. For me, these are two of many ways of experiencing reality. Sometimes I experience the nondual, sometimes the dual, sometimes both together, sometimes I have nothing to do with either. Reality has many ways of experiencing.

So I'm proposing that we respect both points of view. The nondual point of view is a real, authentic way of experiencing things.

The dualistic, scientific point of view is a real, authentic way of experiencing things. Reality can experience itself dualistically. It can experience itself nondualistically. It is much bigger than dual or nondual.

Of Consciousness and Paradox

JEAN HOUSTON

When one studies the nature of spiritual experience, we discover that we are the players in a great game called paradox. And what is the paradox? It is that we are both infinite and finite beings. As finite beings we are Akashic consciousness incarnate in space and time. As infinite beings, we are the living universe in an eternal yet spirited form of itself. As this infinite self expressing aspects of God, and as a form of the living universe, we find ourselves capable of creating and sustaining an individual finite self—that is you, the human being, that is the microcosm, or, if you will, the fractal of the infinite self.

We appear to be separate from the infinite universe, but the new quantum/Akashic physics developed by Ervin Laszlo shows that beneath this seeming separateness there is a deeper unity, a nonlocal connectivity.

We live in a holographic universe where all is connected with all, regardless of where any thought or action is located in time or space. In fact, from my years as a student of spiritual traditions and psychologies, I find that in virtually every tradition, especially in the mystical form of each, when we enter into the depths of ourselves through different states of consciousness, we always find we are connecting with the flow that sustains the entire universe. Therefore we have access to the wisdom, knowing, skill, and transformative power that it contains.

The wisdom of creation is directly accessible to us in our everyday life experience, as the hum of knowing resonance is the core of our being. The universe is an infinitely creative organism that imparts its creativity to us, and we, in turn, reflect this by delivering our creative nature and process to those objects of our creation. These in turn change the nature of the universe, bring new material into the Akasha, which sparks it to still greater creativity. As we cannot contract the infinite to fit into the finite—if we do so we just end up with a fundamentalist God—we can extend through conscious work on ourselves, and service to others, the capacity to expand and enter into partnership with the infinite. Then, and this may be the goal of the paradox game, we do indeed discover that we are infinite selves creating and sustaining our individual human selves but having access to the plans, knowledge, and creativity, and even some of the powers of the infinite self.

The stupendous import of this statement is a mind-cracking, soul-buffeting, life-enlarging realization. Once understood and internalized, it adds tremendous power to our freedom to be, our enormous capacity to grow, evolve, and re-create ourselves, and our ability to live simultaneously as finite and infinite beings. The infinite self has a part in directing the development and unfolding of the finite self, and the finite self offers joy, entertainment, and knowledge to the infinite self. This is the paradox of partnership resolved. The game is to overcome the illusion of separation. It may be the ultimate goal of living in a time of renaissance, one in which consciousness, the ground of all being, is central to the evolution of self and society.

Ultimately the paradox game is about all of us together, as human incarnations of cosmic consciousness, cocreating the ever-unfolding reality.

Be Blissful

ROBERT THURMAN

Recently, I edited a very long, complicated Tibetan book. One thing I learned especially intrigued me: the so-called Buddha nature, which is interpreted in various ways at various levels of Buddhist thought, is really a being who has become every being. How do you become every being? You fall in love with every being.

You see no difference and you feel the feelings of that beloved. Therefore, all you want is for that beloved to be happy, to be free of suffering. The suffering of that beloved is as unbearable to you as your own suffering. There's no question, should I do something about my hand in the fire? Shall I be compassionate to it? No, you just pull it out of the fire. Absolutely, without a moment's hesitation.

Buddha is a being who has become like that for all of us. That is the Buddha nature, the Buddha as us. Buddhas feel that what they call their *dharmakaya*, the reality body, has become all of reality. All of reality includes all sentient beings. All sentient beings includes us. We are, therefore, from Buddha's point of view, the same as he is. From his point of view, or her point of view, or its point of view— there are male Buddhas, female Buddhas, and some third option— they are us. It is said that they are like a mother who considers every being as her only beloved child.

Though each one of us is Buddha looking out at other Buddhas, do we know that? No, we don't. We think we are separate beings, sitting in our separate places. Of course, to each of us, our own self is the most important. That makes us paranoid, because we know other people don't agree with us. Not only do they not think we're the most important, they think they're the most important. This is samsara. This is the struggle of one against another, a losing battle.

This is all I want to share, that this is the best of all possible worlds—it couldn't be better for each of us. We are at exactly the evolutionary place we need to be. Everything that happens to us is just what we need to learn, and nobody gets out of here just by dying. Dying wise means knowing that there is no death, that you just go on. When you have to give up your body—which will happen to all of us, and has happened to us many, many times—you embrace a new one. And the new one is just as good and as beautiful as your openness and generosity, and your ability to give yourself away.

That's what life is: our ability to give ourselves away. Death just stands there as the reminder that we should be giving ourselves away at all times. Of course, nobody really wants us, so don't go jump in anybody's lap, because it won't help. But you should be willing to do so.

In certain moods, in certain states, suddenly everything is really beautiful—every flower, every tree, every blade of grass, even a piece of concrete, even the metal left over from an auto wreck. Anything is beautiful when we're in a certain state—a nondual state. A dual state is where your mind immediately separates you. You believe "That's a bad thing, that's a good thing," and then suddenly everything sucks.

In the conventional, scientific perspective, we think the universe is a bunch of hard objects. Buddha says the universe is made of the intersection of the minds of infinite numbers of beings. In reality, it is voidness, like empty space—but it's not empty space, because space doesn't get in the way of the things that are in it. Nonduality means that the empty space of nirvana, of emptiness, is all of us—all these differentiated things—in this place. The idea that there is a state of bliss somewhere else is wrong. Sometimes it is blissful to be somewhere else, to be blown away somewhere else, but that's not ultimate reality. That's just a relative state. The absolute state doesn't mean that things are nothing or empty. It means that this is

ON THE MYSTERY OF BEING

everything there is. That's nonduality. When you know that totally, then you expand to be all of it, you embrace all of it, you take responsibility for it, and you feel it. Then it's bliss.

We are conditioned by authoritarian cultures. There are two sides. The religious people in this culture tell you that you are sinful, and you need this weird guy who's up there somehow holding out on you. But eventually, after you die, he'll take care of you, so you'll be fine. Wisdom means resignation to the fact that it all sucks. That's what we're told. You're worthless, because you're a sinner.

On the other side, the materialists say, "Well, it sucks because we know it sucks, because we haven't made the right drug for you. We haven't made you into a computer, we haven't made you into a robot so you can be perfectly happy because you're made of metal. Oh, don't worry, it'll be soft metal. It'll be sexy metal, like *Terminator 3*."

That's what you're told; it's the default position in your mind. You don't want to let go, because you think you'll either fall back into nothing—which you hope for, actually—or into pain and suffering. That's what the universe is made of. It's badly made. God didn't have modern technology. God didn't have a PhD from CalTech, so he made a shitty universe. It didn't get made well enough, there's not enough for everybody. So let them all die—the other people—and you'll be fine in your Tesla.

Buddha smiled when he understood the nature of reality, because he understood that, actually, it's a gas. It's nirvana. Here, we're in nirvana. Everyone's made of bliss. That's what you're made of. You don't notice it because it is you, and it's the chair you're on. But all you notice is that this chair is not soft enough. "My butt hurts. I've had to sit here far too long." Your mind is carving this up in a negative way because your culture told you to do so, and you don't realize it.

It's a big effort for those of us brought up like that. It's not just a Western thing. Eastern authoritarian cultures are just the same: all those macho-looking forms of the Buddha they make, who look like everybody's worst bureaucratic nightmare. The Buddha didn't look like that. Buddha was really beautiful. He wanted people to see him as beautiful, because he wanted them to see themselves as beautiful. That's the whole point.

We can keep being reborn stupid, and fight with everybody as long as we want, but we can't avoid being enfolded by a loving awareness that is the ultimate teacher. Somehow everything is well arranged for us. It didn't create our situation, it doesn't have the power to automatically bomb us into bliss, but it has the power to reshape our circumstances, to give us optimal lessons, to teach us how to understand, how to trust our own Buddha intuition, and how to realize that this is joy, and bliss, and happiness, and perfection.

Loving everyone is the only way to go. You must do that, and you feel like doing that when you're blissful yourself. So be blissful.

The Qualitative Science of the Heart

KABIR HELMINSKI

What is it possible for us to know? And how do we know it?

There is a "science" of the heart founded upon the experience of those who have made their own consciousness their instrument of research and experimentation—and who have a highly developed understanding and practice related to the awakening and development of the heart.

Many people have speculated on the spiritual implications of cutting-edge physics. This has given fuel to the belief that we create our own reality. Another inference is that all these energies are not only interdependent but are actually a unified field of oneness. So, from the perspective of quantum and relativity theories, reality would seem to be an energetic whole, more mind than matter.

Some years ago, listening to one of the great quantum scientists, it suddenly occurred to me that in all the talk of science's spiritual implications, we were still talking about a quantitative science developed from physical measurements and mathematical models. The deeper we go into the quantum realm, the more we are dealing with pure mathematics, far removed from sense perception. Our physicists are compelled to use *metaphoric* language to attempt to talk about what their equations imply. As charming as the poetics of subatomic physics may be, let us remember that it is something like poetry. A simple definition of poetry is to say one thing and mean another.

Furthermore, even talk of the mind's influence on reality (thought's influence on reality) neglects an essential aspect of human experience—the human heart, through which we experience our most precious moments and relationships, and through which life itself is valued.

It was as if I had a glimpse of a parallel reality. Side by side with the material universe of measurements was a dimension of qualities experienced by human consciousness. It seemed to me that this magnificent science, based in quantitative measurement and mathematics, is observing reality from the outside. For instance, we can measure and observe that the patterns of electrical activity in the brain of a spiritually developed human being are different from the average human being, but this tells us little about the experience of that human being.

Mere thought is incapable of experiencing reality in its fullness; it is limited to thinking—about thoughts, about physical experience, and even about the heart. However, the heart itself is a cognitive power that experiences a universe of relationships and values, and has a vocabulary of its own for a myriad of heart experiences such as awe, wonder, tenderness, affection, humility, courage, generosity, gratitude. The qualitative science of the human heart has more to do with the experience of being inside, with how that experience can be transformed and deepened, and what that transformation does to the sense of self.

We can become more consciously aware of a dimension of experience known and verified by our own inner experience through a range of subtle, subconscious, and supraconscious faculties. The totality of these faculties for sensing relationships, qualities, and values are described by the mystics of the great traditions as "the heart."

It is through the heart that we experience existence qualitatively, that we are motivated to do what we do, that we are touched and moved by events and situations. All value and meaning is experienced through the heart. In other words, the heart has a profoundly cognitive function, allowing us to experience a dimension of values and qualities side by side with the material universe that is described by the physical sciences.

This observation may seem elementary to our common sense, and yet it seems to have been generally overlooked in discussions of the spiritual significance of quantum science. It is as if a fundamental attribute of consciousness has been overlooked, unaccounted for. The experiences of the heart are not just epiphenomena, the flimsy by-products of the human electrochemical organism. Let's for a moment imagine a "science" that could explore the qualitative dimension of experience, the universe in which compassion, love, and awe are as real as the laws of physical science, a dimension of experience inherent in existence itself.

This is what is meant by the qualitative science of the heart—a science known to some of the great mystical traditions. In philosophical terms, I'm calling for a phenomenology of the heart, the recognition of the cognitive functions of the heart and the possibility that these functions of heart perception can be developed and refined.

Science is encompassing the vast distances of the cosmos, the structures of biological life, and the subatomic realms. As much as we may know about matter and energy through the quantitative measurements of physical science, where will we find an equivalent knowledge of our own inner experience? That qualitative dimension leads us to seek knowledge and to share it with others, and at the end of the day is the dimension where everything we value resides.

As we know, conventional science still has not solved the mystery of what consciousness is, how it arises, and what its purpose is. Some neuroscientists even question whether it truly exists, believing it is a mere illusion created by the brain. Others are curious about the interface between consciousness and the so-called physical world. In a nondual universe, how can we have two distinct realms: one of quantitative scientific measurement and another of human values?

I believe this is the implicit question behind the whole undertaking of "science and nonduality." The accomplishments of physical science and mathematics bring us to a threshold in which matter, energy, and time are interwoven. Matter, energy, and time are like a list of ingredients for cooking the great bagel of the universe.

If the universe is a bagel, who is going to taste it?

Along with the great scientists of history, there have been equally great men and women of taste, of inner knowing, of moral and spiritual greatness. Such people have moved us, inspired us in that highly subjective inner world where we experience the ultimate mysteries of human consciousness: peace, intimacy, love, enlightenment.

In the language of Sufism, the divine oneness addresses the primordial human being, saying: "But for thee I would not have created the universes."

The Anomaly of Consciousness

PETER RUSSELL

Western science has had remarkable success explaining the functioning of the material world, but when it comes to the inner world of the mind it has very little to say. And when it comes to consciousness itself, science falls curiously silent. There is nothing in physics, chemistry, biology, or any other science that can account for our having an interior world. In a strange way, scientists would be much happier if minds did not exist. Yet without minds there would be no science.

This ever-present paradox may be pushing Western science into what Thomas Kuhn called a paradigm shift—a fundamental change in worldview. The shift begins when the prevalent paradigm encounters an anomaly—an observation that can't be ignored but which the current worldview can't explain. As far as today's scientific paradigm is concerned, consciousness is certainly one big anomaly. It is the most obvious fact of life. No one can deny that we are aware and experience an internal world of images, sensations, thoughts, and feelings. Yet there is nothing more difficult to explain. It is easier to explain how the universe evolved from the Big Bang to human beings than it is to explain why any of us should ever have a single inner experience.

The initial response to an anomaly is often simply to ignore it. This is indeed how the scientific world has responded to the anomaly of consciousness. And for seemingly sound reasons.

First, consciousness cannot be observed in the way that material objects can. It cannot be weighed, measured, or otherwise pinned down. Second, science has sought to arrive at universal objective truths that are independent of any particular observer's viewpoint or state of mind. To this end, they have deliberately avoided subjective considerations. And third, there seemed to be no need to consider it; the functioning of the universe can be explained without having to explore the troublesome subject of consciousness.

However, developments in several fields are now showing that consciousness cannot be so easily sidelined. Quantum physics suggests that, at the atomic level, the act of observation affects the reality that is observed. In medicine, a person's state of mind can have significant effects on their body's ability to heal itself. And as neurophysiologists deepen their understanding of brain function, questions about the nature of consciousness naturally arise.

When the anomaly can no longer be ignored, the common reaction is to attempt to explain it within the current paradigm. Some believe that a deeper understanding of brain chemistry will provide the answers; perhaps consciousness resides in the action of neuro-peptides. Others look to quantum physics; the minute microtubules found inside nerve cells could create quantum effects that might somehow contribute to consciousness. Some explore computing theory and believe that consciousness emerges from the complexity of the brain's processing.

Yet whatever ideas are put forward, one thorny question remains: How can something as immaterial as consciousness ever arise from something as unconscious as matter?

If the anomaly persists, despite all attempts to explain it, then maybe the fundamental assumptions of the prevailing worldview need to be questioned. This is what Copernicus did when confronted with the perplexing motion of the planets. He challenged the geo-centric worldview, showing that if the sun, not the earth, were at the center, then the movements of the planets began to make sense. But people don't easily let go of cherished assumptions. Even when, seventy years later, the discoveries of Galileo and Kepler confirmed Copernicus's proposal, the establishment was loath to accept the new model. Only when Newton formulated his laws of motion, providing a mathematical explanation of the planets' paths, did the new paradigm start gaining wider acceptance.

The continued failure of our attempts to account for consciousness suggests that we too should question our basic assumptions. The current scientific worldview holds that the material world—the world of space, time, and matter—is the primary reality. It is therefore assumed that conscious experience must somehow emerge from the world of matter. But as this assumption is getting us nowhere, perhaps we should consider alternatives.

One alternative that is gaining increasing attention is the view that the capacity for experience is not itself a product of the brain. This is not to say that the brain is not responsible for what we experience—there is ample evidence for a strong correlation between what goes on in the brain and the experiences that appear in the mind—only that the brain is not responsible for the capacity for consciousness. It is an inherent quality of life itself.

In this model, consciousness is like the light in a film projector. The film needs the light in order for an image to appear, but it does not create the light. In a similar way, the brain creates the images, thoughts, feelings, and other experiences of which we are aware, but awareness itself is already present.

This alternative paradigm doesn't change anything we've already discovered about the correlations between the brain and experience. This is usually the case with a paradigm shift; the new includes the old. But it also explains the hitherto puzzling anomaly. In this case, we no longer need scratch our heads wondering how the brain generates the capacity for experience; it is already there. The brain merely determines what appears in consciousness.

Radiant Intimacy of the Heart

CYNTHIA BOURGEAULT

When people hear the word "contemplation" nowadays, they tend to register it as simply the Christian equivalent of "meditation." It has something to do with stilling the mind, not thinking, not calculating—"resting in God," in the celebrated formulation of contemporary Christian spiritual master Thomas Keating.

But while this popular revisioning of contemplation has no doubt been useful for getting many Christian practitioners back on meditation cushions, it does represent a substantial diminishment of the original understanding of the term. In the early centuries of Christianity—and borrowed directly from the great philosophical tradition of the Greeks—the real meaning of contemplation is not resting in stillness; rather, it designates a path of *luminous knowledge* of an extremely high order. It's not content-free by any means. It's simply that the content is so high and so densely ordered that it tends to overwhelm the faculties of our usual rational mind, and the mind falls still and silent before it.

"Knowledge impregnated by love" is how John Chrysostom, a sixth-century Christian master, described it. Overwhelmingly, these ancient masters saw contemplation not as a practice for stilling the mind, but as a different kind of mind altogether, something more closely approaching what we would call a level of consciousness.

But why "love"? Why is the Christian tradition as a whole so stubbornly insistent on naming the chief operative in this higher-seeing condition as love? Are we talking here about the emotion of love? It would seem so, if you read through the literature and look at the language used to describe this state. Over and over, the dominant metaphors for it are drawn from the field of erotic love and even nuptial union. But there's a piece here that doesn't often come out in the treatises, or in mainstream theological interpretations. It's all too easy to dismiss the effusive, nuptial language as a sign of perception operating at a dualistic level—but I've actually come to believe that it contains a very different piece of information. And when this piece of information is seen for what it is, it brings a very powerful piece into our understanding of what nonduality is, and how it functions.

"It is only with the heart that one can see rightly. What is essential is invisible to the eye." This well-loved quote from *The Little Prince* is not only a wisdom teaching in its own right, it encapsulates the very Christian experience of the nondual. What if "knowledge impregnated by love" doesn't refer to the emotion of bliss or rapture but rather *knowledge centered in, seated in, and generated by the heart?* Or, even more precisely: knowledge accessible only when the mind is in the heart—to use that phrase so beloved by the ancient masters of the Christian East. And suppose this is not a metaphor but an actual description of a physiology of transformation that becomes understandable only when we come into our own era and have tools, like Levels of Consciousness theory, to help us see what we're talking about.

When viewed through the lens of contemporary models of Levels of Consciousness, contemplation turns out to be the closest equivalent in the Western Christian experience to what's known as nonduality. That's what the entire first half of my book *The Heart of Centering Prayer* sets out to show. Buried in all this effusive and off-putting nuptial language is actually a key piece of information—in fact, *the* key piece of information that the West has to bring to the unfolding dialogue on nonduality.

Nonduality is not, in Christian experience, simply an extension of the cognitive mind. Its signature feature is that "the mind is in the heart," as the masters of the Christian East hammered home again and again. And this statement is no vague or sentimental benediction; it implies, and in fact explicitly stipulates, both a physiology and a pathway of transformation.

"Blessed are the pure in heart, for they shall see God," Jesus announced in his set of teachings traditionally known as the Beatitudes. The tradition of the heart as an organ of spiritual perception flows through the esoteric traditions of the West. It reaches little peaks of particular intensity in the desert fathers and mothers of the fourth and fifth centuries, in Eastern orthodox mysticism, and then, profoundly, in Sufism, which takes the traditions and the teachings of the heart that were the common language of this Western insight and develops them into a highly reformed art.

Throughout this tradition, there's a strong propensity to identify the heart—and yes, I do mean the physical heart—as an organ of spiritual perception. Throughout the early centuries of Christian monasticism, this core insight is faithfully transmitted, together with an accompanying teaching that any fixation on particular thought forms—repetitive, associative, desire-ridden patterns of thinking, or *logismoi*, as the fourth-century desert master Evagrius called them—results in triggering the passions that, in turn, divide the heart, catapulting the unfortunate practitioner out of the realm of luminous seeing and wholeness.

The teaching was, in turn, passed on and developed even further in the Christian East and in Sufism. The heart works as a radiant mirror and a magnifier of a truth, of a knowingness of a different order. As long as it's whole—or "pure," as it's sometimes called, meaning undivided—it can do this. But as soon as it gets co-opted by the so-called "passions"—those tempestuous, stuck emotions that we often perceive as the seat of our emotional selfhood—then the whole thing loses its capacity for seeing. That's the teaching, and in the most profound renditions the goal of learning to see with the heart is always a two-pronged process.

The first is an active spiritual attitude of letting go, a surrender of all attachments—literal, psychological, and, ultimately, perceptual—to objects and thought forms. As Simeon, an eleventh-century Greek orthodox spiritual master, writes in his treatise on three methods of attention and prayer: "You should observe three things before all else. One, freedom from all cares...even about good things. Two, your conscience should be clear so that it denounces you in nothing. And three, you should have a complete absence of passionate attachment so that your thought inclines to nothing worldly." Remember, passion here means stuck emotion; in other words, so that you don't get reactive. That's the practice he lays out. In such a way, and only in such a way, he claims, is it possible to develop a capacity that he calls "Attention of the Heart," the foundational prerequisite for actually being able to follow the teachings of Christ.

Simeon implicitly recognizes that these Christic teachings emerge from a much higher level of consciousness than the ordinary mind can sustain or comprehend. As he says, if you don't have your mind in your heart, it is impossible to do the Beatitudes, to even understand them. In our modern Levels of Consciousness, he's saying that the Christ teaching comes from a nondual level, and you can't run it when you're running a dualistic program.

Lest you get the impression that attention of the heart is merely a spiritual attitude, putting the mind in the heart makes it clear that something much more embodied is being envisioned here. While this veritable mantra of the Eastern orthodox tradition might be misconstrued as advocating emotion over thinking, it's clear from the texts themselves that putting the mind in the heart is not merely—or at all—a devotional attitude. It's accompanied in these texts by specific instructions on concentrating and holding attention in the region of the chest, affecting what contemporary neuroscience would more typically describe as an entraining of the brain waves to the rhythms of the heart. Putting the mind in the heart was then referred to as "vigilance" or "nepsis." Nowadays, it's often understood to mean thinking about the heart, but the Christic texts, again and again, describe bringing warmth down, collecting sensation in the region of the chest, holding it as an embodied accompanying practice to an attitude of letting go of identifications, passions, issues, agendas.

Attention of the heart is not merely a metaphor. It denotes a whole new physiology of perception, without which nondual attainment is impossible. Simeon was saying this in so many words back in the eleventh century. I want to make very clear that this awareness is not absent in the Asian traditions. I vividly recall the story of a Buddhist master being asked how he had arrived at some insight. "My mind tells me," he said, pointing to his heart. The Asian masters may simply never have conceived of separating mind and heart in the first place. But in the Western traditions, and in Western translations of Asian texts, this nuance does not reliably come through, resulting in many maps, such as Ken Wilber's influential Levels of Consciousness, which support the inference that the third tier of nondual consciousness is merely an extension of the cognitive mind into higher realms of spiritual experience.

The Western maps, properly interpreted, make clear why this can never be so. They say that if you're going to run the nondual program of perception, one of the basic physiological requirements is that the whole thing is entrained to the heart and to the specific mode of perception of the heart. I suggest that the sensate experience of the mind and heart is actually the principle explanation for Christianity's stubborn attachment to the realm of the personal. I know this is very frustrating for many Christians. You'll often hear it said in nondual circles that the nondual is nonpersonal, and that access to the nondual realms requires moving beyond the personal. And Christianity's stubborn attachment to the language of love and adoration is often taken as a sign of a religion operating at a lower level of consciousness—still wedded to the personal view of God, not yet fully launched into the transpersonal. But I think something else is at stake, and it becomes clear when you experience attention of the heart phenomenologically. In other words, *what actually happens when you collect attention through sensation in the region of your heart?*

Be forewarned: This is not an easy spiritual exercise. It's all too easy to fall off the razor's edge into either visualization or emotivity. Collecting sensation in the heart depends upon a finely honed capacity to hold attention. It requires patience and it requires practice.

But when you finally arrive at the goal, a literally "mind-blowing" revelation awaits you: namely, that when your attention is gathered in the heart, the felt sense that emerges is one of *pure intimacy*—objectless, radiant intimacy that exudes from the core of the heart without needing an object to attract it. Try it for yourself. Intimacy is what it feels like to look at the world from the point of view of mind in heart consciousness.

Perhaps Christianity's stubborn attachment to the language of the personal has nothing to do with projections onto Big Daddy in the sky, or of egoic pain and pleasure. Rather, consider that every genuine insight and teaching that has ever been generated in Christianity, or in any other tradition for that matter, has been generated in the heart—that is to say, through intimacy. This is how and where mystical perception actually occurs, at least according to the unanimous testimony of the West. The nuptial language simply bears witness to the place of origin. It's a way of authenticating that divine revelation transpires within the domain of heart, under its aegis and agency, making connections not through the cooler logic of metaphysics but through the warmer language of vulnerability, surrender, and belongingness.

PART THREE

Science Embraces Consciousness

Exploring reality through the lenses of science and spirituality has always been an integral part of our journey. While we grew up in different cultures, one common thread has been the constant desire to explore and understand the big questions of life. We both clearly remember the angst, the insatiable curiosity, the constant burning desire to find answers. Whether studying higher mathematics, quantum physics, and evolutionary biology, or creating media on leading scientific theories of consciousness, we both always had the intuition that, by looking more closely through these very different lenses, we would have a more complete picture of who we are and what life is.

According to the great spiritual traditions, consciousness is all there is. Variously called the Universe, God, or Self, it is the ground of all existence. Everything that we experience and perceive arises and subsides in consciousness. The mystics describe the world as made out of consciousness, and matter as a manifestation of consciousness itself. Consciousness is the very process of life in which we are embedded.

For science, consciousness is mostly assumed to be a by-product of the activity of the brain. How electrical signals in the brain translate into the various subjective experiences and perceptions, or "qualia," is still a mystery. Solving this mystery is referred to as "the hard problem" of consciousness. However, there is no real scientific evidence for this assumption, and maybe the hard problem is actually no problem at all—if the issue is approached from a different point of view.

For science and spirituality to come together and help us understand who we are and how we view reality, we need to deeply question many assumptions and beliefs we have held, both in science and in spirituality.

In this section we share some of these pioneering new ways of looking at and studying consciousness. We present theories that attempt to unify mind and matter, and that approach life as a multidynamic, multirelational conscious field in which we are all embedded.

Ultimately, we might never be able to unravel the mystery of consciousness. What unites scientists and mystics is their desire to question, to challenge assumptions, to experience truth, and to live in the awe of the mystery. In that spirit of discovery, in that awe, in the silence of the heart—that is where science and spirituality can really meet.

—Maurizio and Zaya

A Brief History of Consciousness

STUART HAMEROFF

Consciousness defines our existence, but the nature of consciousness remains mysterious, debated since ancient times along two general lines. First, Plato, Descartes, and modern neuroscience have asserted that the brain produces conscious awareness, experience, feelings, and a model of the world, and thus that consciousness emerged during the course of biological evolution. On the other hand, Eastern philosophy, Aristotle, panpsychists, Whitehead, and modern quantum physics approaches[1] have suggested that consciousness is intrinsic to the universe, and that consciousness, or its precursors, have been in the universe all along.

But where, exactly? Panpsychists see consciousness as a property of all matter, but at what level—atoms, nuclei, electrons, protons, neutrons, quarks? At a small scale, particles are in quantum superposition of multiple states or locations simultaneously, then reduce or collapse to particular states (quantum state reduction or collapse of the wavefunction). The natural state of small-scale matter is immaterial, repeatedly becoming material through collapse/reduction, and then slipping back to superposition.

Rather than a static property of matter, as panpsychists contend, could consciousness be in the dynamic collapse process itself, continually updating? Seen thus, consciousness would be a process, a sequence of events, or frames, as suggested by Whitehead, for example.

1   Stuart Hameroff and Roger Penrose, "Consciousness in the Universe: A Review of the Orch OR Theory," Physics of Life Reviews 11(1), (2014): 39-78.

Specifically, Sir Roger Penrose proposed that 1) superpositions were separations in fundamental space-time geometry, 2) that these separations were unstable, and 3) that they undergo spontaneous collapse or reduction to material states at an objective threshold, due to a property in the very makeup of the universe. This is "objective reduction," OR), and each OR event was suggested to result in a moment of simple, "proto-conscious" experience. Penrose's view was in contradistinction with—180 degrees opposite from—the famous "observer effect" in quantum mechanics, that conscious observation causes collapse/reduction, thus putting consciousness outside science. Penrose turned it around. Quantum state reduction (OR) causes, or is equivalent to, consciousness, putting consciousness into science as a natural process in the structure of the universe. Penrose's OR is the only specific scientific mechanism for consciousness yet proposed.

If so, these proposed protoconscious OR moments would have been occurring randomly, separately, everywhere, since the early universe. Each might have some primitive perceived feelings, including, for example, pleasure or pain. In appropriate conditions for pre-biology—primordial soups and thermal vents, for example—organic molecules, perhaps similar to dopamine, might have then accessed a range of feelings, including pleasure and pain, and self-organized to optimize, organize, and "orchestrate" pleasurable feelings as a feedback fitness function—the "quantum pleasure principle." Protein polymers like microtubules developed to resonate, optimize, and orchestrate protoconscious moments into full, rich conscious experience—"Orchestrated Objective Reduction," "Orch OR." As human and animal behavior is based generally on reward, protoconscious pleasure available in the universe may have prompted the origin of life, which then evolved not for gene survival, but to optimize pleasure, or reward. Be it hedonistic, altruistic, or spiritual, life evolved to feel good.

However, quantum approaches to consciousness, including Orch OR theory, were considered unlikely at warm biological

ON THE MYSTERY OF BEING

temperatures. But plant photosynthesis was found to utilize quantum coherence, and quantum resonances in microtubules were discovered at all frequency ranges at biological temperature. And studies on anesthetic gases indicate that the critical factor in selectively erasing consciousness is the dampening of quantum vibrations within the microtubule in the blue-green spectral region. If Orch OR is correct, consciousness may operate as quantum-resonant vibrations in brain microtubules across many scales—more like music than computation. As a quantum process connected to fundamental space-time geometry, consciousness may conceivably occur at deeper, faster scales in the nonlocal structure of the universe, perhaps independent of biology.

Will life continue to evolve to optimize consciousness? Where will we go from here?

Reality Is Eye Candy

DONALD HOFFMAN

Our conscious experiences are quite complicated and have all sorts of unexpected properties. For example, our experiences of color are highly correlated with an area of the brain called V4. If you have a stroke in V4 in the left hemisphere, you lose all color experience in the right visual world—it just looks like shades of gray. If you take a magnet and inhibit V4 in the left hemisphere, you lose color temporarily in the right visual field. Take the magnet away and color comes back.

This is just one of hundreds of correlations we've found. Every conscious experience that we've been able to test has a neural correlate, and this has raised the scientific question: How does matter, perhaps neural matter, create conscious experiences? We have tons of data, tons of correlations between conscious experiences and states of the brain, so how does the magic happen? How does neural activity create conscious experiences?

This turns out to be one of the biggest unsolved mysteries in science today, and it's not new. Gottfried Leibniz raised this question three hundred years ago, and Thomas Huxley raised it in 1869, saying that how neural activity causes conscious experiences is as mysterious as a genie appearing out of a lamp when you rub it. We still don't have any scientific theories that explain how conscious experiences could emerge from brain activity.

This raises the question: Can there actually be a science of consciousness? Can science actually address this question or not? We don't expect monkeys to have the concepts needed to understand quantum mechanics. Maybe Homo sapiens doesn't have the concepts we need to understand how matter could give rise to consciousness. Wittgenstein said, "Whereof one cannot speak, thereof one must be silent."

Then there's the argument from a spiritual direction as well. Rumi said, "Silence is the language of God. All else is poor translation." Science has been very successful, but when it gets to consciousness has it gone beyond what it can do? Is the spiritual realm where progress stops?

Now, I respect someone who says silence is the language of God and all else is poor translation, and then is consistent and says nothing further. I would respect that, but that's not what happens. Tens of thousands of words in every spiritual tradition try to deal with issues of consciousness, and we have conferences where we talk about it. There are lots and lots of words. If we're not going to be silent, then we should at least try to be as precise as we possibly can.

Science is characterized by careful observations, by precise, testable theories, and by the willingness to be shown that you're wrong. Precise theories are precise not because you think you're right, but so that others can tell you precisely why you're wrong. Can we be precise about consciousness so that we can be shown to be wrong?

We can learn by doing careful experiments on conscious experiences. There are things about them that surprise us. We are not infallible about our conscious experiences, and we are not the true authorities on the nature of our conscious experiences. Introspection about conscious experiences is fallible. That's why we need science.

Part of my background is in psychophysics, the science of studying conscious experiences and building mathematical models. We do careful experiments and can write mathematic equations that actually describe the conscious experiences you will have. So conscious experiences can be described by mathematics.

How can we move forward with a scientific theory of consciousness? I think science and religion, science and spirituality, science and nonduality have contributions to make to a new science of consciousness, but there are going to be challenges for science and for spirituality, to do this successfully. Deeply held preconceptions are going to have to be let go to make progress.

Here are the challenges for science. Scientists believe that space, time, and objects exist even if they're not perceived. They also believe that space, time, and matter are the right concepts to describe objective reality. One reason most scientists think that those are the right concepts is because we perceive the world that way—in terms of space and time and physical objects. I want to propose that that's false. Those are the wrong concepts.

There's an evolutionary argument. We don't see all of reality, but those of our ancestors who saw reality accurately had a selective advantage over those who saw it less accurately, so we are the off-spring of those who saw reality more accurately. We might get things wrong here and there, but in general, our perceptions are accurate. That's the standard view, and it turns out that it's false.

When you analyze the equations of evolutionary game theory—which attempts to model strategies and predict results for evolving populations—it turns out that, whenever an organism that sees reality as it is competes with an organism that sees none of reality and is tuned to fitness, the organism that sees reality as it is goes extinct. It's very clear. If our senses evolved and were shaped by natural selection, the probability that we would see reality as it is is zero. The probability that space and time and matter are the right concepts to describe objective reality is precisely zero.

Back in 1633, Galileo said, "I think tastes, odors, colors, and so on reside in consciousness. Hence, if the living creature were removed, all these qualities would be annihilated." He thought that colors and tastes were not objective properties of the world, but sub-jective properties of consciousness. He still believed that physical objects and space-time were objective. Galileo took the first step. There's another step. You have to let go of space, time, and physical objects as well.

Space, time, and objects exist only in consciousness. That's a bitter pill for most scientists, but some are coming around. Nima

Arkani-Hamed is a professor working on fundamental physics at the Institute for Advanced Study at Princeton, and he's come to the conclusion that space-time is doomed. He says that in the underlying description of the laws of physics, there's no such thing as space-time. That's startling because what physics is supposed to be about is describing things as they happen in space and time. If there is no space and time, what is physics about?

Our theories of quantum mechanics and general relativity, which assume space-time, are deeply wrong. We're going to have to give up space-time.

What is space-time and what are our perceptions of objects? I think a good way to think about them is that they are just a user interface. We evolved a user interface.

If you're crafting an email on your computer and the icon for the email is blue and rectangular and in the right corner of your screen, that doesn't mean that the email in your computer is blue and rectangular and in the right corner of your computer. The interface is not there to resemble reality. It's there to hide reality and to give you eye candy that lets you do what you need to do. That's what evolution did: Three-dimensional space is our desktop. Physical objects are the eye candy. They are there not to show us the truth but to hide the truth and let us act in ways that keep us alive. Space-time is not a fundamental reality. It's a data structure that we evolved. We're living in the matrix of our data structure.

When I open my eyes and I have a conscious experience that I describe as "a red tomato one meter away," I'm interacting with something, but that something is not a red tomato and it is not in space and time. It's something utterly different.

And here's the kicker for the problem of consciousness. When I look inside the skull and I have a conscious experience that I describe as a brain and neurons, I'm interacting with an objective reality, but that reality is not brains and neurons. It's something utterly different. The best I can do as a humble member of Homo sapiens is to describe it as brains and neurons. But brains and neurons do not exist, unperceived. They have no causal power, and that's why we've never been able to boot up consciousness from neural activity. It can't be done, because neurons have no causal powers. They're just useful fictions of our desktop interface.

Scientists have to give up the idea that there is a third-person science. The key idea of third-person science is that you can look at this physical object and I can look at the same physical object and we can both make measurements of it and then compare. But there are no public physical objects, and space-time itself is doomed. All of science is first-person science. There can be comparison between different experimenters, but it's all first-person science.

Finally, I am proposing the idea that conscious agents are fundamental. I think we have to reboot science with a notion of consciousness. The story that there was first the Big Bang, and then, billions of years later, life, and then, hundreds of millions of years later, consciousness, is fundamentally wrong. It's the other way around. Consciousness is fundamental. We need a mathematical model of it, and from that model we need to boot up space-time and matter. We can do that, but it's going to take some hard mathematical work.

Now, challenges for spirituality. Everybody's going to have to give up on something here. First is to admit that maybe consciousness can be described with mathematics. The only way to show that this is wrong is to try, and go down trying. Can we come up with a mathematically precise theory of consciousness and, from that, boot up space, time, and matter?

I think a precise mathematical science of consciousness is possible—a science that doesn't have to be a contradiction to human emotions and aspirations. The two can work together. Science is about careful observations and testable theories, and there are no infallible authorities. Scriptures and teachers can be a source of inspiration, but we cannot take them as infallible authorities. For some that might be difficult.

Science and spirituality can work together and bring our insights to make a very human, very rigorous approach to understanding the question of consciousness, so we can finally understand who we are. That's my hope. Science and spirituality, working together, can explore, and I think understand, consciousness.

How to Make a Universe

JUDE CURRIVAN

How does the duality-based appearance of our universe arise from the nondualistic oneness of an infinite and eternal cosmos? In other words, how is our universe "made"?

Explanations of the bridge from cosmic mind to its manifestation have been offered, from ancient wisdom teachings to quantum physics. Yet, only now do I consider the latest scientific evidence sufficiently compelling to offer a radical new understanding of how our universe exists and evolves.

Recent discoveries and insights are enabling the convergence of science and spirituality, embracing an integral perspective on how our universe arises and emerges from non-physical, causative realms of unified reality. This convergence, while ushered in by quantum and relativistic physics, is only now possible, thanks to increasing understanding of the role of information and the so-called holographic principle.

This shows that cosmic mind, articulated as digitized information and represented as dynamic and relational patterns and processes of meaningful information, literally informs the formation of our universe—recognizing the primacy of consciousness, as espoused by Max Planck, Albert Einstein, John Archibald Wheeler, David Bohm, and other pioneering scientists. Physicists know that the physical world is incredibly ephemeral, though apparently solid. An experiment led by Antoine Bérut and Eric Lutz reported in 2012[1] demonstrated the innate nature of information by showing that

1   Antoine Bérut, Artak Arakelyan, Artyom Petrosyan, Sergio Ciliberto, Raoul Dillenschneider, and Eric Lutz, "Experimental Verification of Landauer's Principle Linking Information and Thermodynamics," Nature 483 (2012), 187–189.

deleting one digitized bit releases physical heat, in line with theoretical predictions.

Increasingly compelling evidence[2] is showing that digitized information, the basis for all our technologies, is exactly the same as the universal information that underpins and makes up all physical reality. Pointing to information being more fundamental than energy-matter and space-time, and expressed in complementary ways as these emergent phenomena of our universe, it shows how cosmic consciousness "makes" a universe that exists and evolves as a unified entity.

In addition, cosmologists are coming to recognize that our universe is manifested holographically. This holographic principle posits that digitized information pixelated at the minute Planck scale of the two-dimensional holographic boundary of space projects the appearance of the physical world. The mathematical signature and patterns of this new comprehension are being revealed by evidence at all scales of existence and across numerous fields of research.[3] And the first direct cosmological evidence for its veracity was demonstrated in 2017.[4]

To paraphrase Marcel Proust, the real voyage of discovery is not in seeking new landscapes, but in seeing with new eyes.

This is the case with the growing perception of an *info*rmed and holographic universe. Restating the first and second laws of thermodynamics in terms of information or "infodynamics," and viewing our emergent universe as a cosmic hologram, not only offers a way to reconcile quantum and relativity theories, but shows how the two

2   Vlatko Vedral, Decoding Reality: The Universe as Quantum Information (Oxford, United Kingdom: Oxford University Press, 2010).

3   Jude Currivan, The Cosmic Hologram: In-formation at the Center of Creation (Rochester, VT: Inner Traditions, 2017).

4   Niayesh Afshordi, Claudio Corianò, Luigi Delle Rose, Elizabeth Gould, and Kostas Skenderis, "From Planck Data to Planck Era: Observational Tests of Holographic Cosmology," Physical Review Letters 118 (2017).

laws respectively enable our universe to exist and evolve as a coherent entity and an expression of a unified cosmos.

This requires not new laws of physics or additional mathematical formalism—but for us to see physical reality with "new eyes." We do so by recognizing the physicality and fundamental role of information and considering key attributes of our universe, as follows:

1. Spatially, our universe is geometrically flat, which has been cosmologically demonstrated. Otherwise, the equivalence of energy and matter would be violated and $E=mc^2$ would not apply.

2. The universe is finite in both space and time. No infinite physical quantities exist within space-time, only finite manifestations, including the cosmic microwave background (CMB) wavelength distribution, which has a finite cutoff. Beginning 13.8 billion years ago, most hydrogen in our universe has already been processed into stellar nucleosynthesis. The temperature of ambient space (currently at approx. 2.7 degrees K) reducing to at or near absolute zero also suggests a finite end-time.

3. Space expands.

4. Universal time flows unidirectionally. Otherwise the laws of physics would not be constant.

5. The universe is also closed/isolated in space-time. Otherwise universal conservation of energy-matter would be violated.

6. The universe is nonlocally integrated. Bell's Theorem requires this for quantum mechanics to function, and nonlocal entanglement has been experimentally demonstrated to at least six hundred light years from Earth.

Incorporating the role of information, and based on these key attributes and the premise of the holographic principle, we can now track, restate, and expand the laws of thermodynamics as laws of infodynamics.

The first law of thermodynamics states that the total energy of a closed system is conserved. As our universe is a closed/isolated system and energy and matter are equivalent, this can be restated: The total energy-matter of our universe is conserved. Given that quantum theory is a description of universal energy-matter, this is also its simplest and most generalized statement.

With the evidence that information is physically real and can be expressed as energy-matter, we can expand this to become the first law of infodynamics: Information expressed as the total energy-matter of our universe is conserved. The second law of thermodynamics states that the total entropy of a closed system always increases over time.

As our universe is a closed/isolated system, relative time and space are combined as invariant space-time, and space-time began in a state of lowest entropy, the second law can be restated: The total entropy of our universe always increases over space-time. Given that relativity theory is a description of space-time, this is its simplest and most generalized statement.

Initially investigated by Ludwig Boltzmann, the concept of entropy was originally applied to the behavior of gases and measured the number of microstates of a gaseous system. Its inexorable increase over time led to a common view that it marks an increase from order to disorder. However, building on early insights by Claude Shannon, it is now being viewed by quantum information physicist Vlatko Vedral and others as the informational content of a system. Combined with the holographic principle, it leads to an understanding that universal time flows and space expands to entropically express ever more informational content within space-time. Instead of order to disorder, informational entropy embodies the universal arc from simplicity to complexity. Thus, the flow of time itself is the entropic accumulation of the informational content of our universe.

This leads to the second law of infodynamics, which states: The informational content/entropy of our universe, expressed as space-time, always increases. Essentially, the first law of infodynamics shows how our universe exists and the second law of infodynamics how it evolves as a unified and finite entity—a finite "thought form" in the infinite and eternal mind of the cosmos.

This new perception also explains why space expands. As a fine-tuned Big Breath, rather than the implied chaos of a Big Bang, the expansion of space through the flow of time enables ever greater amounts of informational content, embedded as digitized bits on its holographic boundary, to be projected as the experiential reality of our universe's evolutionary impulse.

In revealing how our universe is "made," this emerging whole-world-view integrates with universal spirituality to confirm that mind and consciousness aren't something we *have*, but what we *are*.

It shows our universe not only exists and evolves as a unified entity—it exists *to* evolve. And as microcosmic cocreators, it verifies that we are part of its evolutionary impulse and share a vital purpose at this pivotal moment for ourselves and for our planetary home.

Mind, Matter, and Life: A Unified Systemic View

FRITJOF CAPRA

At the forefront of contemporary science, a new scientific conception of life has recently emerged. The universe is no longer seen as a machine composed of elementary building blocks. We have discovered that the material world, ultimately, is a network of inseparable patterns of relationships; that the planet as a whole is a living, self-regulating system. The view of the human body as a machine and of the mind as a separate entity is being replaced by one that sees not only the brain, but also the immune system, the bodily tissues, and even each cell as a living, cognitive system. Evolution is no longer seen as a competitive struggle for existence, but rather as a cooperative dance, in which creativity and the constant emergence of novelty are the driving forces. And with the new emphasis on complexity, networks, and patterns of organization, a new science of qualities is slowly emerging.

During the last thirty years, I developed a synthesis of this new understanding of life—a conceptual framework that integrates four dimensions of life: the biological, the cognitive, the social, and the ecological. I presented summaries of this framework, as it evolved, in several books. My final synthesis was published in a textbook titled *The Systems View of Life*, coauthored by Pier Luigi Luisi, professor of biochemistry in Rome.

I call my synthesis "the systems view of life" because it involves a new kind of thinking—thinking in terms of relationships, patterns, and context. In science, this way of thinking is known as "systems thinking," or "systemic thinking."

Systems thinking emerged in the 1920s from a series of interdisciplinary dialogues among biologists, psychologists, and ecologists. In all these fields, scientists realized that a living system—an organism, ecosystem, or social system—is an integrated whole whose properties cannot be reduced to those of smaller parts. So, systems thinking involves a shift of perspective from the parts to the whole. The early systems thinkers expressed this insight in the now well-known phrase "The whole is more than the sum of its parts."

During the 1970s and 1980s, systems thinking was raised to a new level with the development of complexity theory, technically known as "nonlinear dynamics." It is a new, nonlinear mathematics—a mathematics of patterns and relationships. Strange attractors and fractals are examples of such patterns, visual representations of the system's complex dynamics.

During the last thirty years, the strong interest in nonlinear phenomena generated a whole series of new and powerful theories that have dramatically increased our understanding of many key characteristics of life. My synthesis of these theories is what I refer to as the systems view of life.

One of the most important insights of the systemic understanding of life is the recognition that networks are the basic pattern of organization of all living systems. Ecosystems are understood in terms of food webs (networks of organisms), organisms are networks of cells, and cells are networks of molecules. The network is a pattern that is common to all life. Wherever we see life, we see networks. Indeed, at the very heart of the change of paradigms from the mechanistic to the systemic view of life, we find a fundamental change of metaphors: from seeing the world as a machine to understanding it as a network.

Closer examination of these living networks has shown that their key characteristic is that they are self-generating. In a cell, for example, all the biological structures—the proteins, enzymes, DNA, and cell membrane, for example—are continually produced, repaired, and regenerated by the cellular network. Similarly, at the level of a multicellular organism, the bodily cells are continually regenerated and recycled by the organism's metabolic network. Living networks continually create—or re-create—themselves by transforming or replacing their components. In this way they undergo continual structural changes while preserving their web-like patterns of organization. This coexistence of stability and change is one of the key characteristics of life.

One of the most important, and most radical, philosophical implications of the systems view of life is its conception of the nature of mind, which finally overcomes the Cartesian division between mind and matter that has haunted philosophers and scientists for centuries.

In the seventeenth century, René Descartes based his view of nature on the fundamental division between two independent and separate realms—that of mind, which he called the "thinking thing" (*res cogitans*), and that of matter, the "extended thing" (*res extensa*).

Following Descartes, scientists and philosophers continued to think of the mind as some intangible entity and were unable to imagine how this "thinking thing" was related to the body. The decisive advance of the systems view of life has been to abandon the Cartesian view of mind as a "thing," and to realize that mind is a process.

This novel concept of mind was developed during the 1960s by Gregory Bateson, who used the term "mental process," and independently by Humberto Maturana, who focused on cognition, the process of knowing. In the 1970s, Maturana and Francisco Varela expanded Maturana's initial work into a full theory, which has become known as the Santiago theory of cognition.

The central insight of the Santiago theory is the identification of cognition, the process of knowing, in the process of life. Cognition, according to Maturana and Varela, is the self-generation and self-perpetuation of living networks. In other words, cognition is the very process of life. The self-organizing activity of living systems, at all levels of life, is mental activity. The interactions of a living organism—plant, animal, or human—with its environment are cognitive interactions. Thus, life and cognition are inseparably connected. The process of cognition—or, if you wish, of mind—is immanent in matter at all levels of life. For the first time, we have a scientific theory that unifies mind, matter, and life.

Mind and the Wave Function Collapse

HENRY STAPP

From a conversation with John Hagelin at the SAND conference,
October 2014.

The question is, "How is a choice made? Where does it come from?"

We feel that we are individuals, and we feel we have a history behind us, and in our past experience we've made choices—and such-and-such happens. There's a residue of understanding that if I do this, this will happen, and if I do that, that will happen.

We all have this feeling of somehow having an existence. We have a feeling that all of these experiences that we had have melded together to give a feeling of *usness* that involves all these ideas around our personal actions and agency. This makes our choices meaningful.

They're informed choices. They're informed by all your past experiences. You exist, not just as something that's here and now; you exist as a consequence and a product of all the life experiences you've had in the past. And that gives you the feeling of being you. That feeling is, "I know how to do things. I know if I want this to happen." You have this whole feeling of youness, and also the experiences you've had around gaining knowledge.

You have a huge, rich, semiconscious—almost unconscious—knowledge of who you are, upon which meaning can be based. In other words, once you understand yourself as somebody that has these capacities, you can form value. Some things worked better, some things not as well. You can embed in yourself values of *this is good, this is bad.*

You have a conglomeration of feelings that constitute your mental and psychic being. It's on the basis of these feelings of you—who you are, what you are, what you value—that a choice is made. It doesn't come out of the blue. Niels Bohr calls it free choice on the part of the experimenter.

What does free will, or free-willed choices, mean? What it means, in quantum mechanics, is that these choices are not determined by the physical variables, by the physical aspect of nature. It says the mental is coming in here: the feeling of who you are, what your values are, your capacity to do things, what sort of effort needs to be made to cause something to happen. The you that is behind these choices is this complex you, derived from your past experiences.

These choices are meaningful. You've injected meaning into the universe because you have these values and you're an individual that has the capacity to make choices to implement one value and de-emphasize others. These free choices are not something that's coming out of the blue. They're not coming out of the physical world; they're coming out of you as a mental being.

The mind is not just chugging along doing only one thing. Suppose you're walking through the forest and out jumps a strange creature. Your mind is going to be able to create a number of different scenarios for what you might do. Fight or flight.

The brain has a mixture of all the possibilities; it's looking at this array of options for what it might do. It has its values, it has its capacity to make things happen, because of how it learned to relate its efforts to how it acts. It looks and sees this array of possibilities, and it makes its choice.

It has its own dynamics. It is doing mental processing, so it is a mental entity. The brain is generating possibilities, but the mind is made of a different sort of stuff. The brain is described in physical terms, in terms of mathematical properties ascribed to space/time points. On the other hand, we have this mind that is described in psychological terms: sorrows, values, pains, sensations—a completely different language. It's a different sort of entity from the brain. It examines the brain, it's attached to the brain, but you have to think of it in mental terms—some would say even in spiritual terms.

This mental or spiritual part is different from the physical part, and is choosing which option the brain is displaying. That's really where my interest lies. This understanding of the mind/brain connection is what it's all about, as far as I can see. It's a blending of neuroscience and physics—quantum physics in particular.

Idealism Reloaded: The End of the Perception-Imagination Duality

BERNARDO KASTRUP

According to the mainstream materialist paradigm, the world out there is made of subatomic particles and force fields outside and independent of consciousness. This world allegedly has no intrinsic *qualities*—such as color, flavor, and smell—and consists instead of purely abstract *quantities* and mathematical relationships. The qualities of experience, according to this view, are created inside our skull by our brain; living organisms capture abstract stimuli from the external world through their sense organs, and then their brains supposedly translate these stimuli into the experiences that constitute their lives.

The notion that all colors, flavors, and smells exist only inside our heads—instead of in the world out there—is profoundly counterintuitive. The motivation for believing it is the need to make sense of at least two facts: first, that there are strong correlations between patterns of brain activity and inner experience, which seems to implicate the brain in creating experience; and second, that we all seem to share the same world, so if experience is created by our individual brains, there must be something out there that isn't experiential in nature, but that nonetheless modulates the experiences of different people through their respective sense organs. This nonexperiential "something" out there—that is, subatomic particles and force fields—allegedly *is* the world we all share.

The problem is that an increasing array of evidence seems to contradict the notion that experience is somehow created by patterns of brain activity. If this notion were correct, one would expect richer experience to *always* correlate with increased metabolism in the neural correlates of experience. Yet the opposite has been observed.

Indeed, psychedelic trances, which represent unfathomable enrichment of experience, are accompanied only by *reductions* in brain metabolism. Similarly, it has been observed that the brain activity of experienced mediums is reduced as they write or record in the process of psychography. Patients who have undergone brain damage due to surgery have also been observed to have richer feelings of self-transcendence after surgery. Pilots undergoing G-force-induced loss of consciousness also report "memorable dreams," even though blood flow to their brains is reduced. Teenagers worldwide play a dangerous game of partial strangulation, because the reduction in blood flow to their heads leads to rich experiences of euphoria and self-transcendence. The list goes on, but the point should be clear: there are many cases in which brain function *impairment* correlates with *enriched* awareness, which seems to contradict the mainstream materialist paradigm.

To resolve this dilemma, one simply needs a subtle shift in perspective, a different *way of seeing* what is going on. Consider, for instance, lightning. Do we say that lightning *causes* atmospheric electric discharge? Certainly not; lightning is simply what atmospheric electric discharge *looks like*. Similarly, flames don't cause the associated combustion; they are simply what the combustion *looks like*. Finally, a whirlpool in a stream doesn't cause water localization in the stream; it is simply what water localization *looks like*.

These images—lightning, flames, whirlpools—say something about the process they are an image *of*. For instance, we can deduce many things about combustion from the color and behavior of the associated flames. More generally speaking, we say that there are correlations between the process and its image, for the latter is a *representation*—incomplete, as the case may be—of the former.

Returning to the whirlpool example: notice also that there is nothing to a whirlpool but water. You can't lift a whirlpool out of the water. Yet, the whirlpool is a concrete and identifiable phenomenon; one can delineate its boundaries, point at it and say, "There is a whirlpool!" Images of processes can, after all, be very concrete indeed.

So the brain—in fact, the whole body—is merely *the image of a process of localization in universal consciousness,* a localization of experience that, from a first-person perspective, makes up our private inner lives. The body-brain system is like a whirlpool in the stream of universal experiences.

The brain doesn't generate experience for the same reason that a whirlpool doesn't generate water. Yet brain activity correlates with inner experience—the localized contents of the whirlpool—because it is what the latter *looks like* from a second-person perspective, just as lightning is what atmospheric electric discharge looks like from the outside.

The brain is not the cause of experience for the same reason that lightning is not the cause of atmospheric electric discharge, and flames are not the cause of combustion. Just as flames are but *the image* of the process of combustion, the body-brain system is but *the image* of localized experience in the stream of universal consciousness.

In the same way that there is nothing to a whirlpool but water, there is nothing to a living body but universal consciousness. Yet, just as one can delineate the boundaries of a whirlpool and say, There is a whirlpool," one can delineate the boundaries of a living body and say, "There is a body." This explains the felt concreteness of living organisms under the hypothesis that all there is to them is universal consciousness.

This is but a teaser of a much more elaborate theory of reality, developed in a body of work published in the areas of analytic philosophy, psychiatry, neuroscience, and the foundations of physics, which interested readers are invited to explore further.

PART FOUR

The Wonder of Nature

As little children, we feel no separation. Our connection with nature is immediate and profound. Filled with innocence, staring at the stars in a calm night sky perhaps, we got in touch with the immensity of life. Then, as wounds accumulate and the ego began to play its role of survival tool, we lose that innocence.

For us, by early adulthood, there was so much pent-up rage and revolt inside, that our passion for nature turned into environmental activism. Advocating, protesting, bringing awareness to all the ways we abuse nature and exploit it manifested as a deep calling. An activity still run by a righteous ego trying to "do the right thing" or "save the planet," it eventually ran its course and exhausted itself in utter disillusion. Then the pendulum swung to the other side and the quest turned inward. The spiritual quest was all that mattered. There was no space for anything "external." It would take many more years still before the realization landed that there was no such thing as "outside" versus "inside," that spirit and nature were one and the same.

That realization was nothing new for humanity. Indeed, the ancient thinkers and mystics inspired by the beauty and order of nature saw life and spirit in all things and the cosmos as a living organism. Their quest to understand the patterns of nature and our relationship to them inspired a view of life and nature as an intelligent, interconnected whole. Just like their etymology suggests, matter, matrix, and mother were intimately related. From ancient paganism to native American traditions, our spiritual life was deeply rooted in the cycles of mother nature.

With the advent of paternalistic religions—and later, with the so-called "scientific revolution" of the seventeenth and eighteenth centuries—nature came to be seen more and more as an external object of possession and exploitation. Its purpose became to meet human needs. We didn't belong to nature anymore; nature belonged to us. This led to ways of living and relating based on individualization and separation. Cut off from the nurturance of our mother, humans felt both special and unique and, at the same time, alone, fragile, and anxious in a hostile universe.

The science emerging today has come full circle. It supports the ancient Stoic idea that the universe, and matter itself, are intelligent and self-organizing. Furthermore, the boundaries we believed in, between "us" and "our environment," are found to be false. On a microscopic level, bacteria vastly outnumber human cells in our own bodies; we cannot live without them. At the molecular and atomic levels, our boundaries get still more diffuse. All the atoms we are made of were once part of the planet; some were formed in a supernova explosion billions of years ago.

Looking through the lens of emerging science, we come to realize that nature, far from being a static environment in which we exist and evolve, is an unfolding, dynamic process, characterized by the power of transformation. Our bodies are not separate entities; they extend throughout the whole of nature. This realization can trigger a deep emotional connection, a profound somatic understanding that our bodies are not where we begin and end, and nature is not located outside of us. It provides us with an embodied perception that we are not separated from anything else in life. As the mystics have told us for centuries, we don't live in the universe; the universe lives in us.

As our bodies become more attuned to the cycles and patterns of a living universe, we become more available to respond from that understanding of oneness and wholeness. Earth becomes our body. If it hurts, we hurt. We no longer take care of the planet from a place of righteous indignation, but simply from a deep realization that we are taking care of ourselves. The deep reverence and awe we feel when looking at the stars is the same feeling we have for life, spirit, and ourselves, confirming once again that nothing is separate.

—Maurizio and Zaya

Fundamental Awareness: The Universe Twiddling Its Thumbs

NEIL D. THEISE

As in so many discussions of the nature of consciousness, we begin with the so-called "hard problem of consciousness." How is it that conscious beings are aware of qualia, like the color of red or the taste of sugar—the experiences of consciousness? In the absence of any confirmation of our cultural belief that mind is a product of brain, scientists and philosophers must still speak of the "neural correlates of consciousness," without ever being able to prove causation.

Approaches to understanding consciousness and to exploring ways to explain the hard problem fall into three domains of human knowledge, investigation, and experience, which we wish to integrate into one framework. First, there's Western philosophy. Though current trends in Western philosophy tend toward the materialist side of things, there is a very deep and broad strand of thinking, from Plato through Spinoza to Kant, Hegel, and Whitehead, saying that mind is everything, that the world of things is not the thing itself; the thing itself lies behind the world of things or under the world of things, or is reflected through the world of things.

In the second domain, contemporary science, there is the central notion of the quantum-mechanical view of the world in what Niels Bohr described as "complementarity," often demonstrated by the famous double slit experiment that shows that the nature of existence depends on how it is observed. So a beam sent through a double slit in a screen will reveal the beam to be either particles or waves, but only one or the other. Both are "true" aspects of the system, but they can never both be captured simultaneously. At the same time, both views must be encompassed to have a complete understanding. Thus, they are complementary.

I often use this kind of illustration to further convey complementarity:

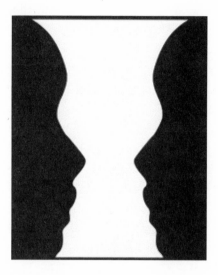

Is it two faces or a vase? You can't see the two faces and the vase simultaneously. You can move very quickly between them, but you can't see them both at the same time. A complete description of this image requires both the faces and the vase, but your perspective only allows you to see one or the other. This is another form of complementarity. Bohr predicted that there would be complementarities in the biological realm and at the cosmological scale, in addition to the quantum level, though he did not see those revealed in his lifetime.

Quantum physicists were confident and comfortable with the notion that consciousness is fundamental. Einstein, famously, was not, though he provided us with two very important related concepts. First, the equivalency or complementarity of energy and mass ($E=mc^2$). Then, the notion of space-time. These concepts meet in the notion of the "quantum foam." Physicists describe the quantum vacuum of space-time not as completely empty, but as an energy-rich field. Since energy and mass are complementarities, the energy of the field will erupt into particles, usually in matter/antimatter pairings that then self-annihilate. This bubbling up of mass from energy, which then subsides back into energy, is the "quantum foam."

However, some of the smallest bits of erupting mass escape that self-annihilation. When they do, they interact with other small things (strings, according to string theory, something else according to other models) and then self-assemble into subatomic particles, larger subatomic particles, atoms, molecules, and so on. This notion of "self-assembly" brings us to another strand of contemporary scientific thought that is relevant to consciousness, along with its related concept of "emergence."

Complex systems theory describes how interacting agents self-organize into unplanned, adaptive, higher-level structures through a process of "emergence." Think of how ants create large-scale structures (food lines, nurseries, cemeteries, farms) through their local interactions "on the ground," without any high-level, system-viewing organizer. It is bottom-up rather than top-down. Complex systems at all levels of scale display similar behaviors: ants, people, birds, plants create colonies, cities, flocks, or forests. These can all self-assemble into ecosystems. Downward in scale, cells self-assemble into tissues, organs, and organisms. Cells are self-assembling molecules, which are self-organizing atoms, which are self-organizing subatomic particles, and so on down to the quantum foam.

This brings us to the biological and cosmological scale set of complementarities, because now we see that all complex systems exist in hierarchies of complex systems (or *holarchies,* as Arthur Koestler called them). If you see an ant colony in the distance, it looks like a solid *thing.* It may be changing shape or moving around, but it looks like a thing. But when you walk up close you see that it's not a thing at all; it's just a community of ants self-organizing. And since the ant bodies are themselves made of cells, when you go closer to the ant and view it at the microscopic level, the ant as a thing disappears and becomes an interactive dance of the cells that make it up—a *phenomenon* rather than a *thing.* Thus, we have another form of complementarity: at one level, every living thing looks and behaves like a thing, but at a lower scale the thingness disappears and the system reveals itself as a phenomenon arising from smaller things.

And so, when the universe is considered across all scales, from all perspectives, there's no object, no *thing*, that has inherent existence. Like the two faces and the vase, every thing is both a thing, from one perspective, and a phenomenon, from another. This is a direct correlate of the Buddhist concept of "the emptiness of inherent existence."

Is the quantum vacuum where everything begins? Maybe, and there are scientists and theoreticians who believe that. But is there another possibility? An answer to this question is proffered by the third of the domains mentioned above: the practices and knowledge of metaphysical/mystical traditions such as, but not limited to, Buddhism, Shaivism, Jewish mysticism, and Vedanta. All of these traditions point to a ground of being that is comprised of pure awareness that is nondual—that is, without a subject-object split.

If we take the experiences and insights of these traditions seriously as data, not as fantasy, then we can posit that if this pure awareness becomes aware of itself, a process emphasized in Shaivist thought, the nondual becomes aware of "a this and a that," or "an I and a that." As differentiation *within* awareness proceeds into a true subject/object split, separation arises, in space and time. All of a sudden you have space-time, that energy-rich field, which in turn emanates the quantum foam—and the whole universe springs into existence. This view is compatible with the Western philosophies and contemporary sciences mentioned above.

To return to the opening question of the hard problem of consciousness, and quoting from an earlier paper: "[T]his integrative framework suggests that a proper understanding of human qualia reflects that qualia are not a "hard problem" to solve, but the foundational nature of all existence. All views and experiences are, in fact, nothing but qualia within the awareness that is the ground of existence. Every field, every wave particle, every atom and molecule, every living and non-living aggregate of such, anything and everything observed, experienced, or imagined, is in fact nothing but qualia within the awareness that is the ground of experience. In this view the human brain is not the creator of our conscious experiences, but the transducer of the fundamental, nondual, nonmaterial consciousness into our own, personal, human minds."[1]

A final implication of this framework is that boundaries have no inherent existence either. My finger stops at my skin, at this everyday level of scale. At the microscopic level, my body is 10 percent human cells and 90 percent bacteria, all of which are necessary to make this human body. At the cellular level, we are a cloud of the microbiome, being deposited on our environments, being shared between organisms. At the molecular and atomic levels our boundaries get wider still. There is no atom in your body that you didn't eat, drink, or breathe from the planet. We are beings that both live *on* the earth and *are* the earth, having self-organized into beings that think and talk about the nature of existence. More sublimely still, we don't live in the universe; the universe isn't an empty space or box. We *are* the universe, arising from its substance. In Buddhist terms, the "relative" and the "absolute" reflect this complementarity; we are both these separate beings in the universe—the relative— and the universe that is seamless and perfect as it is—the absolute; nirvana and samsara are not two—but not one. Going about our daily lives, we are the universe twiddling its thumbs.

1   Neil D. Theise and Menas Kafatos, "Fundamental Awareness: A Framework for Integrating Science, Philosophy, and Metaphysics," Communicative and Integrative Biology (2016).

Rethinking the "Dumb Random Universe" Model of Existence

ROBERT LANZA

Adapted from Beyond Biocentrism, *by Robert Lanza with Bob Berman, published by BenBella Books.*

Biocentrism builds on quantum physics by putting life into the equation. The result is a rethink of everything we thought we knew about the nature of the universe. Biologists describe the origin of life as a random occurrence in a dead universe, but we have no real understanding of how life began or why the universe appears to be exquisitely designed for the emergence of life.

According to the current standard model, the random laws of chance produced everything we observe. Atoms slammed into other atoms. Billions of lifeless years passed with the cosmos set on "automatic" until, on at least one planet, life began. That's the story. Everyone has heard it. Yet everyone can feel how empty and unsatisfying this narrative is. We cannot fathom how lumps of carbon and drops of water acquired a sense of smell.

Subscribers to the "dumb random universe" model—meaning almost everyone—state that absolutely everything arose by chance. It seems reasonable. Chance also makes it appear plausible that a cosmos as numb and insensate as shale could come up with hummingbirds by randomness alone.

The dumb universe paradigm requires that we explain the complex physical and biological architecture we see all around us by some means other than "God." And "chance" is all we have. The dumb universe model sinks or swims on the life raft of randomness.

Randomness is also a central key of evolution, where it works splendidly. Darwin wasn't whistling in the wind with natural selection. It's obvious that giraffes developed long necks because those giraffean predecessors who received random mutations for longer necks had a survival edge. They could grab leaves and fruit from higher branches. Over time—and it doesn't take terribly long—selection of longer-necked animals gave them a leg up.

Evolution works, and it's based on random mutations coupled with natural selection. That being so, we make the mistake of thinking "chance" is the explanation for everything. This includes the entire universe—from the laws of nature themselves to the arising of life and consciousness.

Chance is a process that is misunderstood. The most famous illustration is the monkeys-and-typewriters thing. We've all heard it. Let a million monkeys type randomly on a million keyboards for a million years and you'd get all the great works of literature. Would this be true?

About ten years ago, some wildlife caretakers actually put a bunch of typewriters in front of a group of macaques to see what would happen. The animals typed nothing. Instead, they threw some of the machines on the ground and used them as toilets. They didn't create any written wisdom whatsoever.

But let's carry out a thought experiment. Could a million monkeys typing for a million years truly create *Hamlet*? Believe it or not, such a problem is entirely solvable. Keyboards have a lot of places to push—fifty-eight keys on a typical typewriter. Let's consider the difficulty of creating merely the fifteen opening characters of *Moby Dick*, "Call me Ishmael." How many random tries would be needed?

Given fifty-eight possible keys, it would take about 283 trillion trillion attempts. But remember, we have a million monkeys working. And let's say they type forty-five words per minute, and they never stop to rest or sleep. How much time would it take for one of them to type "Call me Ishmael"?

ON THE MYSTERY OF BEING

Answer: About 36 trillion years! Or more than two and a half thousand times the age of the universe.

So a million monkeys typing furiously would never even reproduce the opening three words of a book. Forget the dumb-universe thing. It's bogus.

But back to our question: Can you get the cosmos we see—including the complex biological designs of the brain and the trumpeter swan—by the random collision of atoms alone? If randomness requires thirty-six trillion years to type a single three-word passage, the answer is obvious—not a chance.

But even if we ignore all this, there's a more serious problem. It turns out that our universe has an exquisite set of properties that are Goldilocks-perfect for life to exist. We live in an extraordinarily fine-tuned cosmos, where any random tweaking would prevent any kind of life from existing. If gravity was 2 percent different, or if you changed the power of the Planck length or the atomic-mass unit, you'd never have stars such as the sun, or life.

So, by any stretch of wishful thinking, a cosmos that allows life is inconceivable by chance alone. Randomness is not a tenable hypothesis. Truth be told, it's close to idiotic—right up there with the dog ate my homework.

Let's sum up the most basic do-or-die physical conditions for life to come into existence. First, two fundamental forces—electromagnetism and "the strong force"—must have specific values. Electromagnetism keeps electrons attached to atomic nuclei, allowing the existence of atoms. But atomic nuclei won't hold together without a perfectly tuned strong force, which allows protons to cling together. Without multiple protons, the only element that could exist would be hydrogen. And while no one is anti-hydrogen, it couldn't produce any kind of organism—even if you waited eons.

Then, you need a third fundamental force—gravity—to not be too weak or too strong, or you couldn't have stars. I could keep going, but suffice to say that around two hundred physical parameters must be exactly as they are—within a percentage or so—in order for stars to undergo nuclear fusion and create their warmth. Or for planets to form, or for all the elements to be created.

In short, yes, it is a perfect universe. And we haven't even yet gotten to the "life-creation" business, with its own crowded stadium of requirements—such as worlds that are not too hot or cold. Or radiation-filled. Or the specific properties of key elements—like oxygen and carbon—that need to exhibit just the characteristics we observe.

Even here on Earth, life would be near impossible if we didn't possess our massive nearby moon, because the axial tilt would wobble wildly—sometimes aiming straight at the sun, producing impossibly hot temperatures.

And how did we get the moon—the perfectly timed collision of a Mars-sized body coming from a very specific direction and at exactly the right speed. Unlike all the other major moons in the solar system, ours is the only one that orbits around its planet's equator. If it orbited "normally" it wouldn't stay in our orbital plane and exert its torque in a sun-vector alignment where it stabilizes our axis.

This is an extremely unlikely universe. So unlikely that even the most die-hard physicists concede that the cosmos is insanely improbable in terms of its life-friendliness. This hyper-unlikely nature—just on a strictly physical level—makes many physicists sigh with discomfort and admit that some sort of scientific explanation is badly needed.

If we apply Occam's Razor—that is, the principle that the simplest explanation is usually the correct one—biocentrism offers the most obvious explanation for our improbable life-friendly universe. Why? To me, the answer is simple: the laws and conditions of the universe allow for the observer because the observer generates them. Duh!

The Origin of Life and Consciousness: Lifting and Gifting Our Collective Future

BRUCE DAMER

Science is on the verge of one of the greatest discoveries of the twenty-first century: we may soon know how the living world emerged from the seeming chaos of the cosmos. If our predictions are experimentally confirmed, we will come face to face with the progenote, the deepest common ancestor of life on Earth. The progenote will not only inform us about how life can begin, but may also reveal how the earliest living entities had the power to shape probability and share resources and information in a way that ultimately led to the emergence of consciousness.

At the age of sixteen, Albert Einstein engaged in a thought experiment in which he ran alongside a beam of light, leading to his later derivation of the theory of special relativity. As a similarly dreamy teen, I began my quest to solve the riddle of the origin of life by visualizing a self-organizing bundle of molecules. For forty years I strove to answer the challenge posed to me by that bundle: "Figure out how I made a copy of myself!"

In late 2013, working in collaboration with Professor David Deamer at the University of California, Santa Cruz, part of the answer flowed into my consciousness. We had been focusing our work on pools connected to hot springs in volcanic geothermal sites, a hotter and more active version of the "warm little pond" that Charles Darwin wrote about as the place where he thought life could begin. In earlier studies, Deamer had shown that as the pools fluctuated between dry and wet states, trillions of tiny, soap-like lipid-encapsulated protocells budded off from layers of dried lipid that formed a ring along the edges of pools. Within those layers, some of the building blocks of life (delivered on micrometeorites from space) could stitch together into RNA, DNA, and peptide polymers, which were then captured within the budding protocells.

We observed how some protocells were disrupted by environmental stresses, but some were stabilized by their polymer cargo, to deliver their contents back for another dry-wet round. That was when I had the revelation that when protocells settled into moist aggregates as the pool dried down, this community of protocells would begin to interact and collectively adapt to selection challenges such as sheer forces or changes in temperature and chemical composition. I visualized that over many such dry-wet-moist cycles the functions of biology could emerge, like the booting up of a chemical operating system. My mental explorations landed at the critical juncture where advanced protocells accidentally combined these functions into a mechanism to divide themselves into viable daughter cells, and the first living microbes came into existence.

While preparing for my talk at the 2017 Science and Nonduality conference, another thought experiment showed that the protocells cycling in the pools resembled an engine operating through three drivers: a probability enhancer, "P" (the crowding of molecules within the protocell); an interconnected network, "I" (the population of protocells sharing resources); and a memory system, "M" (short genetic polymers that write and read instructions to synthesize the next generation of polymers).

I then realized that this cycling P-I-M system might actually be the engine of creation, continuously generating everything that emerges into the living world, including human society, culture, economy, technology, and even conscious experience. I realized that this cycling engine continuously emanates a sort of motive force, shaping low-probability possibilities into actual occurrences and thereby generating ever-increasing complexity.

ON THE MYSTERY OF BEING

As the human mind has emerged on the substrate of the living world, it is a massively complex example of a P-I-M system, and therefore a potent probability-shaping machine. From this insight I offer the following: What if our minds, intimately connected through our sensory nervous system to the larger world, have a much greater power to shape the future through intention—matched by action—than we have presupposed? Could this be an explanation for the ever-increasing pace of synchronicities and seemingly miraculous events that infuse our lives and our world? And could we use the power of clear intention to actively shape a future of desirable, yet seemingly improbable, outcomes? Such a tool could well be the key to our survival.

Another outcome of this work is that humanity may be on the threshold of confirming that life must have begun through a form of symbiosis—that our common ancestor was not a single cell but was instead a community in collaboration. This goes well beyond an abstract concept: the earliest fragile protocell could not have survived on its own, but must have been a part of a much more robust protocell progenote aggregate. Progenotes begat the microbial mat, which for billions of years evolved in mutually beneficial consortia, transforming the Earth to support the rise of complex life.

This discovery has the potential for cultural transformation similar to Einstein's theory of relativity, which helped usher in the modernism of the 1920s, or Copernicus's heliocentric universe, which unshackled the philosophical and religious dogmas of the sixteenth century. The deeply divisive language of Herbert Spencer's nineteenth-century term "survival of the fittest," which Charles Darwin begrudgingly adopted, has justified violence and instilled a sense of separation in society, and no longer serves us or our world.

Perhaps this can be replaced by a new narrative to live by: that evolution actually works by a process of *lifting*, through adaptation to selective challenges, and then *gifting* the resulting innovations to the next generation. Individuals' efforts (and sacrifices) enable the community to progress. This *lifting and gifting* narrative of our evolution and current situation is a more constructive beacon to guide us through treacherous waters into a bright, increasingly collective future.

As we look back in wonder at the astounding miracle of our creation, we may be consciously waking up to the fact that we are living within and must serve to protect this most rare and beautiful progenote planet.

Resurrecting Real Magic

DEAN RADIN

There are four kinds of magic: Fictional magic like Harry Potter. Fake magic like Harry Houdini. Marketing superlatives like "Magic Baby Shampoo." And then there's *real magic,* which I argue is the authentic power that underlies the enduring fascination of the other types of magic.

Real magic is sometimes spelled "magick," to distinguish it from the other meanings. It involves practical applications of an ancient worldview generically known as the esoteric traditions. A synthesis of both Eastern and Western esoteric ideas reveal that the esoteric worldview is what a philosopher would call idealism—the notion that everything is composed of mind or consciousness, including matter. By contrast, the scientific worldview is based on the philosophy of materialism, exactly the opposite of idealism—the idea that everything is composed of matter (or, after Einstein, energy), including mind.

The educated world today has adopted materialism as its preferred cosmology, largely because of the undeniable success of technologies spawned out of the scientific worldview. But because materialism is diametrically opposed to idealism, in the academic world it is only acceptable to talk about magick as fictional or fake. Proposing that magick is actually real deeply challenges the prevailing worldview, and such proposals are regarded as heretical. While the worst consequences of heresy have vanished, and one may no longer be threatened with being physically charbroiled, the inflammation caused by espousing heretical ideas can quickly reduce one's academic career to ashes. Are such dramatic reactions justified?

There are many practices that fit under the umbrella of magick, but all of them fall into three main categories: divination, manifestation, and theurgy. Divination refers to perceptions that transcend the usual constraints of space and time. Historically, these practices include prophesy, astrology, mirror-gazing, tarot cards, and the I Ching. Manifestation involves the use of focused attention and intention to influence the world around you. Common practices include spell-casting, affirmations, and prayer. Theurgy involves evoking spirits and inviting them to do things on your behalf. Its practices are most closely associated with ceremonial rituals, but it also includes the common religious practice of intercessory prayer.

Before I address the question of the reality of magick, let me add that my perspective on this topic is that of a scientist, and not of a mystic or closet occultist. I've worked for nearly four decades in university, industrial, and nonprofit research facilities, specializing in experimental studies of the nature of consciousness and its capacities. I've published nearly a hundred articles in peer-reviewed scientific journals, and another two hundred in magazines. I've written four popular-science books, and I've given more than four hundred presentations and interviews to the general public, academic, government, and military audiences. I use the tools and techniques of experimental psychology, psychophysiology, neuroscience, statistics, and physics in my daily work, and I do not doubt that science is the most accurate worldview that humanity has developed so far.

Why, then, am I proposing that magick should be taken seriously? The answer is simple—because the experimental evidence demands it.

Consider an article from the May 2018 issue of *American Psychologist*,[1] the flagship journal of the American Psychological Association (APA), entitled "The Experimental Evidence for Parapsychological Phenomena: A Review." The author was Etzel Cardeña, professor of psychology at Lund University in Sweden.

---

1   Cardeña, E. (2018, May 24). The Experimental Evidence for Parapsychological Phenomena: A Review. American Psychologist.

After analyzing ten classes of experiments exploring various psychic effects ("psi" for short), Cardeña's conclusion was unequivocal: "The evidence for psi is comparable to that for established phenomena in psychology and other disciplines."

One class of experiment is the ganzfeld telepathy experiment, which uses a mildly altered state of consciousness to enhance subjective awareness of subtle psychic impressions. In a typical ganzfeld telepathy experiment, a "sender" is given a photographic target and asked to telepathically send it to a "receiver," who is strictly isolated by distance and shielding. After the sending period, the receiver is asked to select which of four possible photos the sender was trying to send. Under this design, if telepathy did not exist, the best she could do would be to select the correct target one in four times, for a 25 percent hit rate. But after 108 published studies, consisting of more than four thousand individual test sessions, the overall hit rate was 32 percent—a seemingly modest increase nevertheless associated with odds of ten thousand trillion to one.

A second class of experiments is known as presentiment tests. These measure unconscious fluctuations in human physiology, variables such as heart rate, skin conductance, pupil size, or electrical brain activity, before the participant is exposed to a randomly selected stimulus. Would the body unconsciously respond emotionally before an emotional stimulus, like a photograph of a car wreck, whereas before a calm stimulus, like a plain wooden table, it would remain calm? Because the future stimulus was selected purely at random from a large pool of possible stimuli, one would predict that the physiological measure would on average be about the same before the emotional versus the calm targets. After twenty-six of these experiments were published, a meta-analysis found that the overall odds against chance were one hundred million to one.[2]

2   Mossbridge, J., Tressoldi, P., & Utts, J. (2012). Predictive physiological anticipation preceding seemingly unpredictable stimuli: A metaanalysis. Frontiers in Psychology, 3, 390.

A third class of experiments, called implicit precognition, is a time-reversal effect based on an idea borrowed from social psychology, called priming. In a conventional priming study, you are first shown an emotional word like "happy," and then you see a photo with either happy or sad content. You are asked to press a button as soon as you decide that the emotions of the word and photo either match or mismatch. People tend to be faster when making decisions about primed emotions that match the subsequent photo than with emotions that mismatch. In the implicit precognition experiment, this temporal order is reversed. The photo is shown first, and then the priming word is shown. The idea is that the priming word shown *in the future* will influence how fast the initial decision was made. A 2016 meta-analysis of ninety repeated experiments exploring this time-reversed effect resulted in odds against chance of more than a billion to one.[3]

These and other studies indicate that the practice of divination has been experimentally confirmed, not within the context of esoteric lore, but through the best methods that science can presently provide. Similar examples can be provided for the practices of manifestation and theurgy.

While we are not likely to see major universities offering master's degrees in magick, all this suggests that science is slowly overcoming past prejudices, and that magick is being resurrected. This does not represent a regression to a primitive, prescientific past, as some may fear. Rather, it indicates that some ancient ideas about the nature of reality persist because they've proven to be useful. In the process of revisiting, testing, and refining those ideas, we will undoubtedly reconceptualize many aspects of magickal lore and develop new ways to understand these phenomena.

In this sense, the resurrection of magick is just part of the evolution of the Age of Enlightenment. The first phase of that age, which

3   Bem D, Tressoldi PE, Rabeyron T and Duggan M. Feeling the future: A meta-analysis of 90 experiments on the anomalous anticipation of random future events. F1000Research 2016, 4:1188.

occurred during the sixteenth and seventeenth centuries, provided scholars with a way to escape from the superstitions of medieval and ancient times by focusing on the external, physical world. That period of history was critical in helping to "disenchant" our world-view and break the dogmatic strangleholds that were fiercely enforced by religious authorities. The second phase, Enlightenment 2.0, may be about reenchanting the world by addressing what Enlightenment 1.0 left out—namely, the role of consciousness in the physical world.

Let us hope that this is the case, because one of the unintended side effects of seeing reality through a disenchanted lens is the broad acceptance of a nihilistic and unsustainable worldview—a world-view that is pushing us to the edge of annihilation. Perhaps the Age of Enlightenment 2.0 can help us gain a new perspective of reality that is more life-affirming.

The Mycology of Consciousness

PAUL STAMETS

There are twenty-two primates that are known to consume mushrooms—twenty-three including humans, as we are primates. Goeldi's monkey consumes twelve times its body weight in a year. They know the difference between edible and poisonous mushrooms, and are dependent upon them for sustenance. This speaks to a very ancient, broad knowledge of the co-evolution of fungi and animals, and the co-evolution of fungi and primates, leading to us.

Between two million and two hundred thousand years ago, the human brain doubled or tripled its capacity. In an evolutionary context, that's quick, so what caused the human brain to suddenly expand?

I want to resurrect Terence and Dennis McKenna's Stoned Ape theory. Our hominid ancestors, due to climate change, came out of the trees and crossed the savanna. What did they find? Scat. What is the largest common mushroom in the subtropics, growing in poop? The potent psilocybin-containing mushroom *Psilocybe cubensis*. The majority of the primates eat grubs. Insects lay eggs in mushrooms. Primates seek out the grub-infested mushrooms, eat them, and suddenly they have an amazing expansion of consciousness. They share it with their friends and family. The floodgates open up, and it leads to neurogenesis, the building of new neurological pathways.

Psilocybe cubensis grows in elephant dung, as well as that of hippopotamus, zebra, and many other ungulates. As a hominid, you would quickly realize that these mushrooms give you an extraordinary state of mind. Psilocybin degrades into psilocin, which tightly binds and activates serotonin receptors, stimulating neurogenesis.

It's a serotonin agonist. It substitutes for serotonin, and in doing so, opens the senses to a cascade of stimuli that would have given our primate ancestors a visually rich experience they would never forget.

In 1957, across millions of households in America, *Life* magazine was delivered with a very good psilocybin mushroom field guide, embedded within an article by R. Gordon Wasson, on his adventures in Oaxaca in pursuit of magic mushrooms.

Decades later, I named the most potent psilocybin mushroom in the world, *Psilocybe azurescens*. Up to 2 percent of psilocybin and psilocin within the dried mass of this mushroom are psychoactive crystals. Why would a mushroom produce so much? We don't know, but it's certainly attracted the interest of humans. Psilocybin dephosphorylates into psilocin, and when you ingest these mushrooms, psilocin becomes a temporary neurotransmitter, creating a heightened state of awareness.

Psilocybe baeocystis is another species that's hidden in the landscape. It contains a compound called baeocystin, which is not illegal; it's pharmacologically active, and the methyl group is easily cleaved by normal enzymes. Cleaving off those methylated groups is a normal part of your digestive system. I think the potential of baeocystin should also be examined.

A number of clinical studies were conducted on this. Johns Hopkins published one of the first pioneering articles, showing a mystical-like experience with a relatively high dose of psilocybin that had significance fourteen months post-ingestion. Positive experiences were reported by 70 percent of the individuals; 30 percent reported negative experiences. Interestingly, for those who had negative experiences, the negative experience did not extend beyond the experience itself.

Family members, loved ones, and associates of those who had positive experiences noticed a significant change in the personality of the individuals who ingested psilocybin. And the subjects, remembering the experience long afterward, still reported continuing benefits—the opposite of what happens with posttraumatic stress disorder (PTSD), where you may become retraumatized when you remember the trauma. Remembering the positive experience of psilocybin conferred a demonstrable benefit long afterward.

Another extraordinary study was a survey of prisoners. When 480 thousand people were surveyed by the Department of Social and Health Services, they found that those who had a psilocybin experience were associated with a 27 percent decrease of larceny and theft, a 22 percent decrease of property crime, and an 18 percent decrease of violent crime. Association is not necessarily causation, but it might be. In the couples studied, if a man had experienced psilocybin, there was a statistically significant negative correlation with spousal abuse. (It did not cross-correlate with women.) Men who had tripped on mushrooms tended to be nicer to their spouses. I think that is extraordinarily interesting.

There is a big movement right now for the decriminalization of psilocybin in California and Oregon, and elsewhere in the United States. It comes down to this simple argument: You have a right to choose how you die. Do you want to die in fear, anger, hopelessness, anguish, and regret? Or do you want to die knowing that you're one with the universe—at peace, understanding the unanimity of being? That's a real choice, and psilocybin can give you that choice.

I want to mention microdosing. Microdosing is taking a subthreshold dose of psilocybin, below that which you can feel—about a tenth or twentieth of a gram. I know all sorts of people who would never consider tripping on psilocybin, but for whom the concept of taking a microdose that could increase neurogenesis, and fight depression and senility and dementia—well, that's a whole different thing.

When the FDA was approached by a group of scientists reporting that psilocybin is good for PTSD for war veterans, the FDA told them, "No, this is good for people suffering PTSD from many forms of trauma, not just for veterans." The FDA scientists said they'd never seen a drug so powerful, with so much benefit and with such low potential for abuse. This is not like marijuana or alcohol, where you want to get high the next day, or have another beer. After you trip on these mushrooms, the next day you look at them and say, "Nope! I'm done for a while." They have no potential for abuse.

There's another mushroom called Lion's Mane, which is legal. It's a potent neurostimulant, and it regenerates myelin on the axons of nerves. There have been two clinical studies on this, and both report significant increase in cognitive function after consuming encapsulated mushrooms for about twenty-five days—about four to six grams split into two doses, once in the morning, and once in the evening.

Lion's Mane causes neurogenesis and, in particular, it removes amyloid plaques. There are two interesting studies with mice, which were injected with a toxic polypeptide that induces amyloid plaque formation. Amyloid plaque interferes with neurotransmission and its formation is associated with Alzheimer's patients, and with the degeneration of myelin.

After ingesting the toxic polypeptide, the mice developed full-blown Alzheimer's-like symptoms, with amyloid plaques. Three to four weeks after being fed the Lion's Mane mushrooms, these plaques had resolved. Not only was the amyloid plaque largely removed, they were then able to navigate a maze nearly normally, where previously they had been confused. There were both microscopic and behavioral improvements.

Lion's Mane is a really important mushroom. We all suffer some type of neurological decline with aging, so as a society there is a collective loss in our body intellect, a loss to our cultural knowledge. It's important that we give that knowledge to the next generation, who will become elders in turn—so it is significant that we can decrease neurodegeneration, increase our intelligence, and retain our cognitive function into old age.

The Ecological Initiation

CHARLES EISENSTEIN

Human-nature dualism says, among other things, that human beings are the only full selves in the world. The rest of life is a scum of bio-chemistry atop a rock, devoid of intelligence, consciousness, and full beingness.

I'd like to discuss an alternative: the living planet view. It says that Earth is a living being. This has important consequences, from perception to relationship to policy.

What prevents us from fully taking in the ongoing ecological tragedy? What enables us to read about the destruction of the Amazon, or the dying of the last Northern White Rhino, or the extinction of thirty thousand species a year—and go on with life as normal?

I ask this not as an accusation, but from curiosity. One of the reasons that we have trouble receiving that information into our feeling bodies is that we live in an ideology that says that Earth (or any ecosystem or species) is not a subjective perceiving, feeling, hurting, loving being. Therefore, you could ask the naive question, "Why should we care about nature? Why should we care about the Amazon?"

Here's my cell phone. Why should I care about it? Why shouldn't I just leave it out in the rain?

You say, "Well, Charles, it's very useful to you. That's why you should care about it. And if you leave it out in the rain, then you'll lose your data and have to buy a new one."

And I'd say, "You're right. I should take good care of it."

It's natural to answer the question in that way when we don't see it as an actual being worthy of love. It'd be weird if I said, "I love my cell phone. Not just because it's useful, but for its very being. I sing it lullabies before I put it on airplane mode." That's insane, because we all know it's not a being in that way.

If we ask, "Why should we care about the Amazon?" we are given answers like, "Well, because of the economic value of its ecosystem services, or all those medicines that we can make from the plants, or its carbon sequestration, or its production of oxygen." When we give a utilitarian reason that amounts to "here is how it will benefit us," we are essentially casting it into the same category as a cell phone.

At first, climate change seemed like good news to environmentalists, because finally we could say, "Ah, now they're going to *have* to do what we've always wanted. Otherwise, bad things will happen." But in adopting that narrative, we've replaced love with fear. We have substituted a smaller revolution for a deeper revolution. The ecological crisis is asking us to step into a revolution in our basic relationship to the rest of life—to no longer see ourselves as destined to impose our intelligence onto a natural world that has none, but instead, to see ourselves as participants, contributors, and partners in an evolutionary process bigger than ourselves.

When we see Earth as alive, we begin asking questions like, "What does the Earth want?" We are then moved to care for Earth beyond its use to us, harking back to the early days of environmentalism, when no one was saying, "Save the whales, because if we don't, terrible things will happen to us." It was, "Save the whales, because they are so beautiful. Because they are sacred. Because they are beings. We love them." To step into that is a revolution of love.

The living planet view leads to different priorities. Seeing Earth as alive, we understand that its health depends on the health of its organs and tissues: rainforests, mangrove swamps, grasslands, coral reefs, elephants, whales. We understand that if we cut down the Amazon and compensate for the lost carbon sequestration with a giant array of solar panels, Earth will still die from organ failure. This principle is not easily encompassed in carbon metrics.

You have probably heard about the precipitous decline in insect biomass around the world. It's tempting (though erroneous) to blame it on climate change. Because once we have a cause, then the solution is obvious, too. Find the cause and fight it. Find the enemy, destroy the enemy. Find the terrorists, kill the terrorists. Find the criminals, kill the criminals. Disease? Find the germ. Overweight? Suppress the appetite.

That works in a linear system, but not in a living system. What is the cause of the honeybee collapse? Is it killing the bears that were scratching the trees, which oozed sap that fed fungi that carried antiviral compounds to the honeybees? That's part of a whole matrix of cause. The cause is everything. From the living planet view, we're invited to release reductionistic war thinking.

When we accept the livingness of Earth, we have something to love again, and we no longer have to ask why. We have an alternative to arguments appealing to self-interest, and we no longer need to bribe or scare people into caring—which produces, at best, a simulation of caring. Real care comes, of course, from love. I'm advocating a story, a way of seeing Earth, that gives permission to trust what is innate to us, which is our love of life and our desire to serve it. This is inherent to our humanity.

Let's face it, the corporate-government elites, with their media, their money, their armed forces, their surveillance apparatus…in conventional terms they have the power. If they are irremediably evil, it is hopeless. But are they? The story we hold about somebody creates an invitation for them to step into that story. Can we hold a story that invites a change of heart?

What blocks that innate love of life? What trauma, what ideology, what system? Exiting the good-versus-evil formula for "fighting climate change," we are in new territory. We don't know what to do—which is an improvement over thinking we know what to do, but actually not knowing what to do.

ON THE MYSTERY OF BEING

The intense polarization around the climate change issue sometimes leaves people confused when they read what I have written about it. "Hold on. Which side are you on?" In a fight, that is the most important question. But what if both sides are ignoring deeper assumptions that they hold in common, which are at the root of the problem? In this case, both sides tend to reduce environment to a question of global warming. Which side am I on? Neither and both. I am not fully confident in the conventional narrative and the computer models that project runaway warming. I think it's much more likely that we'll see climate derangement, as the organs and tissues of Gaia lose their vitality and are unable to regulate planetary physiology. We could see rapid warming, or cooling, or wild fluctuations. We already see vast disruptions in the hydrological cycle, floods and droughts that are caused by soil degradation and deforestation.

I ask you to give a moment of attention to your innate knowledge that Earth is alive, and to your readiness to receive the help that you might need to truly know that. Intellectually, I believe Earth is alive, conscious, and intelligent, and the whole cosmos, too. Intellectually, I've accepted that. But the programming is so deep, I need help to undo it.

Together we give attention to our readiness, to our willingness to receive the information that opens us up, and then to be carriers of that information, and walking invitations into the story of love.

PART FIVE

The Body as Teacher

A common pitfall on the spiritual path is to focus on transcendence, while disconnecting from the body. Indeed, many spiritual traditions seem to invite the student to disidentify with the body, through different practices and teachings. If misinterpreted, these teachings can lead to denying the body and the wisdom encoded in it. This not only greatly limits our experience of life, but also makes our spiritual path narrower as we disconnect from our life force, our vitality.

While our search matures, we may experience a distinct transition as we descend from the lofty realms of transcendence back into the body. All of a sudden, all the teachings and realizations we previously experienced and perceived in intellectual form become solidly anchored. We realize they were already living in the body. Along with this descent comes a deeper surrender to life in the immediacy of each moment. No matter what the experience—illness, trauma, anger, bliss, or ecstasy—they all arise as a flow of sensations devoid of interpretation or story.

As much as we love our spiritual teachers in the flesh, the situations we confront moment to moment become our everyday teachers. The tenderness in our chest, the tingling in our belly, the trembling of our voice—these become our teachers. Inside our bodies we explore the essence of billions of years of evolution. We track traces of the pain, fears, and hopes of our ancestors and we connect with the intelligence of life itself. We realize that our bodies are collections of thoughts, experiences, and sensations moving through us at dazzling speed, constantly changing. It becomes apparent that we can never fully comprehend, only feel.

When we put all understanding, all knowledge aside and listen to the body, each sensation becomes a unique portal through which we enter into a deep silence and intimacy with all things. Enlightenment is intimacy with any experience that arises in this human form.

In this section, we share some beautiful portals to the intelligence and wisdom encoded in our bodies.

—Maurizio and Zaya

What Are Our Bodies?

CHRIS FIELDS

We all have bodies, but what are they?

Having a body is the most familiar experience in the world. We all know what it's like, because we each have one. Our bodies are always there, and we know them intimately and well. We regard our bodies as deeply personal. We naturally treat our bodies as unique, special, and most important, *ours*. We have an almost irresistible sense that we live inside our bodies, but even when we feel outside of our bodies, they still feel like they are *our* bodies, not no one's and not someone else's. All of our bodies have gone through enormous changes since our birth, but they remain, while we inhabit them, our own. The idea of having someone else's body is disquieting and maybe even repulsive.

How we relate to our bodies is one of the oldest philosophical questions, and its answers inform entire metaphysical world views. If I decide that I *am* my body, I will naturally be attracted to physicalism. If I think that my body is a thing that I inhabit and animate, I will be attracted to Cartesian dualism. If it seems to me that I only imagine my body, I will tend toward idealism. Within these broad outlines there are many variations advocated by different philosophical traditions, such as dualists who believe they inhabit many bodies in sequence through some process of reincarnation, or dual-aspect monists who believe that they and their bodies are "two sides of the same coin."

What happens, however, when we allow ourselves to question the feelings that we have about our bodies and the metaphysical intuitions that come with them? Our feelings of pleasure, pain, good health, or uneasiness, our feelings of controlling, acting with, and owning our bodies, our feelings of knowing, existing, or having a fixed identity, are all highly malleable by our state of arousal, our emotions, by what is happening around us, and by food, drink, drugs, pathogens, and other input from the environment. How these experiences are produced and how they are affected by various internal and external influences is a major area of research in cognitive neuroscience, and much has been learned about the body-experience link over the past two decades. Experiments and clinical studies show that people can expand their sense of what "counts as" their bodies or lose the sense that parts of their bodies are theirs. Sufferers of Cotard's syndrome even insist that they are dead or do not exist.

Do we have any basis for granting our "internal" experiences of our bodies any more epistemic force than our "external" experiences of the world outside them? Some experiences *feel* more compelling than others, but feelings of knowing are themselves experience, and are often wrong. Even pain can be illusory; it may hurt like hell without our bodies being damaged. From the brain's perspective, the rest of the body is just part of the world—an important part, but one from which attention can be distracted when it is needed for even more important topics.

Let us consider, then, a fairly radical hypothesis: that our feelings of intimacy with our bodies may be essentially illusory. Setting our essentially automatic acceptance and privileging of our intuitions and feelings aside, even just temporarily, allows us to consider alternative perspectives on what our bodies are. The impersonal perspective of evolutionary and developmental biology, which views humans as organisms among many others and human bodies as individuals related by descent from other individuals, offers four ideas about our bodies that directly challenge some of our deepest personal intuitions:

✿ Our bodies are multi-species ecosystems. About 90 percent of the cells in our bodies are bacterial. Bacteria inhabit almost every part of our bodies. We provide

ON THE MYSTERY OF BEING

them with food and a protective environment, and they help us digest our food, regulate our hormonal systems, and, most important, defend us from pathogens.

🪷 Our bodies differ only slightly from those of all other animals, including insects and even sponges. Our genes are very much like their genes, so similar that many human genes work just fine in cells of yeast. Most human neurotransmitter families can be found in sea anemones.

🪷 Our bodies are not individuals, but are rather parts of a huge individual that we call "life on Earth." All of our bodies, and the bodies of all other organisms, are continuous with that of the last universal common ancestor of all of life, and hence with each other. We share not just our genes, but our entire physical selves, with all other living beings.

🪷 Our bodies are aware on many levels, mostly in ways unrelated to "our" awareness. Sometimes the cells, tissues, and organ systems of which our bodies are made are acting in our best interest, but they don't know that. From their points of view, they are acting in *their own* best interest. They are each aware of their own environment, an environment that is mainly inside us. They know nothing of our environment or our perceptions, ideas, or emotions.

What, then, are these bodies that we seem to inhabit, which are also inhabited by millions of bacteria? What are these organisms that feel like they are *ours*—or maybe even like they are *us*—but that are really just parts of the giant, four-billion-year-old living being that is life on Earth? What does it mean to say that we experience the world with or through our bodies, when every part of each of our bodies is having its own experiences, experiences that are nothing like ours? What are we to make of our intuitive feelings of ownership and control of and intimacy with our bodies, when what these feelings tell us about our bodies just seems wrong?

Learning more about our bodies shows us just how little we know about them. It also helps us respect and love them more deeply.

The Essence of Yoga:
Exploring Our True Body

ELLEN EMMET

A little girl runs down a street. Warm air caresses her skin, and the pounding of feet and earth bring an intoxicating counterpoint to the expanding of her heart. Her body unravels like threads of light into the surrounding space, and she melts into its open embrace. The liquid, dancing world anoints her vibrating body with its loving substance...

We have all experienced blessed moments in which our true nature of undivided and universal awareness resounds at the emotional, tactile, and sensual levels of experience. Our body is almost transparent, without borders, suffused with a subtle quality of vibrating intensity and sensitivity. It is impersonal yet intimate, and shares its substance with all that is experienced.

For most of us, however, the everyday body that we wake up with has been deeply and lastingly conditioned by the belief that "I" refers to an individual person, limited in time by birth and death, and located inside a body, separate from other bodies and from the world out there. Corresponding to and echoing this belief, the feeling of the body has become a set of repetitive psychosomatic habits and an intricate web of tensions and density. This creates feelings of solidity, cohesiveness, emotional inertia, and contraction, designed to perpetuate the projected image of the "I" that seems to live at its center, with the past and future on either side. The dynamism of such a body is ruled by the complex and restrictive impulses to protect, defend, or affirm itself.

In this way, the body-mind seems to become the envelope or cage in which "I" appear to live, and the stuff that "I" seems to be made of, while the real "I" of undivided awareness has shrunk itself into confinement, limitation, and fragmentation.

When we touch our true nature of awareness in the presence of a teacher, a teaching, or an intuition, we submit our rational thinking mind to the pure light of intelligence that is its source and substance. With limitless awareness as our invisible reference, we hear and understand that ordinary awareness, "I," is not contained within a body or located in time and space. We hear and understand that "I" is the open awareness in which all experience arises, unfolds, and dissolves—including thoughts, sensations, feelings, and perceptions (mind, body, and world). We hear and understand that this awareness is not a perceived experience, yet is that which perceives all experience, and is not an object, yet is found at the center of all experience as its only, invisible substance.

My identity fits not in any name or form. Nor am I held captive between birth and death. I am not the blood that runs through my veins, nor the warm breath that flows through my nostrils, nor the mouth that breathes. I am not the memory of myself, nor the hopes that skip like stones into the future. Past and future ripple through me as the wind of time, while space is the echo of my infinity. I am not this, yet I am the lover of all things, and find myself at the heart of all that has name and form.

In the yoga of nonduality, we deepen our exploration of our essential nature to include the level of feelings, tactility, and perception. Taking our stand as the field of openness in which all experience arises, we listen to our experience of the body directly, as if for the first time, free of any labels, evaluations, comparisons—without any mediation from the past or any agenda for the future. We take our time, descending below the threshold of rational experience, allowing thought to relax in the background while opening to the flow of tactile sensation that is our actual bodily experience. In time we may be invited to feel that the body of sensation arises in, flows through, and takes itself back to presence or awareness, my true self—as does all experience.

When the welcoming of the body is open, it is as if the body, like a frightened animal, feels an unconditional invitation to come out into the open space. In this friendly, loving field, the body stands naked and undefended, and naturally begins to liberate what it had been holding in and as itself: the crystallized energy of separation that lives as layers of contraction and tension in the cellular, muscular, skeletal, and nervous systems of the body.

As the body unravels in this way, the "me" charge that lives embedded in its layers is returned to the openness of awareness. Gradually and effortlessly, the body is left free to relax into and reunite with the openness that surrounds it. It is as if each feeling and sensation, like an offering, gives itself back to the invisible altar of awareness, telling its true story on the way. In time this allows a gentle and natural realignment with the felt understanding that the body's essential nature is this very openness.

Over and over in this exploration, using guided meditation, postures, visualizations, movement, and breath, we are led to see and feel that in truth we cannot say that a sensation appears in "my" body, or that a sound appears in the world out there, or that a thought is to be found inside the head. We see rather that sensation, thought, and sound all appear in myself, unlocated, without any separate individual existence of body, mind, or world.

Over and over again, we realize that, like sounds and thoughts, the bodily feelings and sensations are subtle in nature. They are not solid or tangible and cannot be held or measured. Rather, they are like vibrating ripples on the surface of myself, intimately one with myself, made of my own invisible substance. We feel and know that the body is the openness that I am.

Unlike most of the conventional yoga practices that are taught in the world, nondual yoga is not a pragmatic endeavor intended for the physical or energy body to increase well-being, strength, flexibility, or to encourage expansive states of consciousness. Rather, it is a sacred practice that surrenders the body back toward its source of open awareness: what we only and always are.

Every time the offering is made, the body is returned as it truly is— limitless, transparent, relaxed, easeful, and loving. It is realized as the very breath of the universe.

The Cerebrospinal Fluid and I Am

MAURO ZAPPATERRA

Fluids come together, and the I Am appears… What is the primary imagination? It is this—I-Amness. The touch you have of the consciousness of your beingness. That is the primary dream. The unimaginable has imagined: Oh, yes—I Am!

—Nisargadatta Maharaj

Our awareness—of *I Am, our beingness, our presence*—begins to develop from our earliest moments of existence, when we are bathed in amniotic fluid in our mother's womb. Immersed in this primordial fluid, the developing brain folds in on itself, encasing the amniotic fluid inside the brain and transforming it into the cerebrospinal fluid (CSF) we carry within us today. Thus, the brain and spinal cord are immersed in, and organizing around, fluid in the womb as we are becoming aware of *I Am*.

Physiologically speaking, CSF is a clear fluid that bathes the brain and spinal cord. It is located both inside and outside the brain and spine and travels all the way to the sacrum (or sacred) bone. The entire central nervous system (CNS) is immersed in CSF.

It is thought that the CSF system evolved as a way to receive signals from the environment, which allow the nervous system to function. For instance, the "brain" cells of sea stars making contact with seawater resemble the early neural cells of a developing embryo. Over time, the body plans of primitive life-forms gradually became enclosed. Sea worms, for example, contain seawater inside and outside of their body, and the two fluids mix—not unlike the way the CSF and amniotic fluid mix in the womb, prior to closure of the neural tube.

Evolutionarily, seawater is the first internal fluid environment of the primitive brain. The brain cells that contact the surrounding fluid have the special role of receiving and transforming information from the fluid (seawater, for the sea star, or CSF in vertebrates). We can say that our ancestral CSF is seawater.

CSF contains a dynamic array of changing proteins, growth factors, and other molecules, and performs multiple roles as it transports nutrients and hormones to the CNS. It facilitates fluid homeostasis in the CNS; eliminates waste; regulates circadian rhythms and appetite; provides guiding cues for neuronal cell migration; supports and protects the CNS throughout embryologic development into adulthood; provides essential survival and growth factors to the embryonic and adult brain; and creates a fluid niche for neural stem cell survival, proliferation, and differentiation.

Interestingly, CSF also contains extracellular matrix proteins, some of the same proteins that make up the connective tissue of the body. CSF is like fluid connective tissue, a liquid matrix for energy and information to be held and transported. CSF carries information within the fluid, whether it is a protein, a growth factor, or a hormone, and transmits that information to the brain. It is a fluid conductor of information.

Could CSF be a transmitter of energy to the body?

CSF operates via volume transmission, which permits information to be simultaneously dispersed without synapses to multiple key brain regulatory centers. The fluid nature of CSF means it can work through resonance as well. Hence, any signal can be transmitted through the fluid and synchronize the tissues. In short, CSF may serve as a vehicle for signaling to major control centers in the brain and transmitting source energy, chi, or prana to the body and the felt sense of *I Am*.

ON THE MYSTERY OF BEING

Some traditions believe that source energy may be transmitted through a "step-down" process, via condensation, or differentiation, from the unmanifested source to our physical self. In Taoism, this would be depicted as differentiation from the Wu Chi (the Void) to the Tai Chi (the Ten Thousand Things)—all one energy but with various forms of manifestation. As this energy condenses, it becomes differentiated and visible to the human eye as physical form.

According to certain beliefs, the initial "step" into the body occurs at the third eye, or the brow center. This is the location of the third ventricle, or space, in the center of the brain, which is full of CSF. It adjoins the pituitary gland in front, the pineal gland in back, and the thalamus and hypothalamus on the sides.

The pineal gland makes direct contact with the CSF and releases information into the fluid for volume transmission to the rest of the brain and body. This space has been called the Crystal Palace and the Cave of Brahma. The Crystal Palace is thought to be an alchemical space that contains the Crystal Water, which when activated anoints the crown chakra and becomes illuminated.

Could the CSF be the conveyer of the unmanifested energy to the manifested physical body? Could the CSF be the liquid medium through which there is an embodied, felt sense of I Am?

Similarly, could the CSF be the transporter of the same primal energy in kundalini? Kundalini is a Sanskrit word meaning "coiled up." In yogic theory, kundalini is a primal energy located at the base of the spine, some say residing in the sacrum, like a sleeping serpent waiting to be awakened. In yogic practice, kundalini is "awakened" and physically moves up the central canal of the body, the shushumna, to reach the third eye and, subsequently—for awakening to occur—the crown chakra.

Interestingly, the word kunda in Sanskrit is translated as "water pot" and may refer to a small lake or pond. CSF fills both the sacrum and the spinal cord, so it is possible that the primal energy "sleeping" in the sacrum could be "awakened"—the CSF activated—and through volume transmission, ascend the central canal of the spine (shushumna) into the third ventricle (third eye).

Imagine this: a dispersal of the life force energy within the fluid, with the CSF as the fluid conductor of this source energy to our physical body. Imagine the brain simultaneously bathed with the differentiated energy from the source, providing the synchronous, unified experience and awareness of our true essence. Imagine the CSF transmitting the experience of *I Am*, our beingness. Connect to your CSF, to your own fluid body, to your liquid light, your prana, your chi, to the structured, resonating primordial ocean within you.

Lessons from the Body

LARRY DOSSEY

As an internal medicine physician, I have spent my professional life listening to messages from the body. In fact, the practice of medicine depends utterly on what the body has to say. Let's consider two cases.

Barbara Cummiskey developed symptoms of multiple sclerosis in the 1960s as a fifteen-year-old high-school student. Although she was an athletic gymnast, she began to struggle physically. She managed to graduate high school in 1968 and enroll in college, but was unable to complete her studies because of increasing disabilities. Her disease progressed rapidly. She had two respiratory arrests in the early 1970s, contracted pneumonia, and required recurrent hospitalizations. One of her lungs collapsed in 1980 and she required a tracheostomy. She lost urinary control and required an indwelling bladder catheter. She further lost bowel control and an ileostomy was performed. Her vision deteriorated and she became legally blind. By 1981 she was given six months to live and was enrolled in hospice care. She became bed-bound, developed severe contractures, and was curled in a constant fetal position. When she could no longer swallow, a feeding tube was inserted into her stomach. She was dying. When death appeared imminent, her family and her doctor agreed there would be no CPR or other heroics to prolong her life.

On June 7, 1981, her tragic story was aired on WMBI, a local radio station. During the program, prayers were requested for her and other terminally ill individuals in the area. Listeners responded enthusiastically and flooded the station with bags of letters.

The same afternoon, with visitors in her room, Barbara heard a male voice say, "My child, get up and walk!" Her visitors were astonished when she jumped out of bed, removed her oxygen, and stood on her legs for the first time in years. She was no longer short of breath without oxygen. Her vision returned. Her parents entered the room. She appeared transformed. Her mother looked her up and down and exclaimed, "You have muscles again!" Her amazed father waltzed her around the room.

That night, a Sunday, she went with her family and friends to church. She walked from the back of the sanctuary down the central aisle to the front. Everyone knew she had been close to death. They were shocked.

The next day, Barbara went to the office of Thomas E. Marshall, MD, her internal medicine physician. Dr. Marshall said:

> I thought I was seeing an apparition! Here was my patient, who was not expected to live another week, totally cured. I stopped all her medication and took out her bladder catheter, but she wasn't quite ready to have the tracheostomy tube removed until another visit. No one had ever seen anything like this before. That afternoon, we sent Barb for a chest X-ray. Her lungs were now perfectly normal, with the collapsed lung totally expanded with no infiltrate or other abnormality that had existed before. I have never witnessed anything like this before or since...

Her case is reported by Dr. Marshall in physician Scott J. Kolbaba's 2016 book *Physicians' Untold Stories*.

In the 1990s I was peripherally involved in the investigation of an equally startling case dating to the 1950s, which was being revisited by a reporter for *The Washington Post*. I had written the book *Healing Words*, and the reporter wanted my opinion. The case concerned Ann O'Neill, a four-year-old girl suffering from acute lymphocytic leukemia. Ann was hospitalized in the University of Maryland Hospital in Baltimore. She was close to death. Her burial gown was prepared and a priest had administered last rites. She was given only hours to live.

Unwilling to give her up, her mother, with the help of several Catholic nuns, bundled her up and took her to a local cemetery, where Elizabeth Ann Seton, a revered Catholic nun, was buried. Ann's mother and the nuns laid her at Seton's tomb and prayed that she would be healed. Then they took her back to the hospital.

Several days later, all of Ann's blood tests were normal. She gradually recovered and was discharged from the hospital. Nine years later, a bone marrow biopsy was performed, revealing no indication of any lingering leukemia.

In both cases, a profound healing of a near-lethal disease occurred following healing intentions from outsiders. In both instances, the healing intention was prayer, an endeavor whose main characteristics involve compassion, caring, and love, commonly offered from a distance. Evidence has surfaced over the past few decades suggesting that the physiology of humans and nonhumans can be modified by these interventions.

Whatever you call it, the bottom line is that the thoughts of one caring individual can positively influence a sick individual at a distance, even when the recipient is unaware of the effort. Distant healing has been demonstrated in scores of laboratory studies in the past few years, and systematic and meta-analyses affirm that the effect is real.

Currently the majority of medical schools in the United States have formal coursework exploring these findings. This indicates that we are moving toward a postmaterial view of human consciousness—consciousness unconfined to the individual brain and body, and capable of exerting distant, nonlocal effects. This perspective sees consciousness as *fundamental*—not produced by the brain, or derived from anything more basic.

This view has been affirmed by some of the most influential physicists of the twentieth century. Max Planck, the founder of quantum mechanics, observed, "I regard consciousness as fundamental. I regard matter as derivative from consciousness." Erwin Schrödinger, another Nobel Prize–winning physicist, agreed: "Although I think that life may be the result of an accident, I do not think that of consciousness. Consciousness cannot be accounted for in physical terms. For consciousness is absolutely fundamental." More recently, mathematician-philosopher David Chalmers stated, "I propose that conscious experience be considered a fundamental feature, irreducible to anything more basic…"

The implications are enormous. If consciousness is nonlocal, as evidence suggests, then it is unbounded and is *infinite* in space and time. If consciousness is unbounded in time, it is eternal and immortal; and if it is unbounded in space, then it is omnipresent, unitary, and one.

The recognition of unitary consciousness is ancient. It is also modern. As Schrödinger put it: "To divide or multiply consciousness is something meaningless. The category of *number*, of *whole* and of *parts* are then simply not applicable to it." And as the eminent physicist David Bohm observed, "Deep down the consciousness of mankind is one. This is a virtual certainty…and if we don't see this it's because we are blinding ourselves to it."

When bodies respond to the healing intentions of distant others, it affirms our unity and connectedness with one another. This permits a reformulation of the golden rule, from its customary "Do unto others as you would have them do unto you," to "Be kind to others because in some sense they *are* you."

The human body, sensitive to the love, compassion, empathy, and healing intentions of others, and in cahoots with all other minds that are themselves infinite and eternal: What greater lesson than this?

The Body, the Medical System, and Modern Society

GABOR MATÉ

The modern medical paradigm separates the mind from the body and separates the individual from the environment. It has a strictly biological perspective.

Suppose you have asthma. What happens in asthma is your airways are narrow and become inflamed, so the airflow becomes obstructed. You are wheezing and gasping for oxygen. They give you medication. It's a biological process; the medication suppresses the inflammation and opens up the airways. This approach is necessary and, insofar as it goes, it's accurate.

However, it's also hopelessly narrow. There is much more to asthma than a biological process in isolation. For example, it has been shown that if you're a black woman in the United States, the more episodes of racism you suffer, the greater your risk of asthma. And, if you're a child, the more stressed your parents are the greater your risk of asthma. In fact, you can almost predict whether a child needs more or less medication depending on how stressed or depressed the parents are. There's an epidemic of asthma right now in North America.

That raises the question: Is asthma simply a disease of the airways—we call it "reversible airway disease"—or is it a disease of the whole person who is suffering stress, or is it a disease of the family system through which the stress is transmitted, or is it a disease of the society that creates racism and that in general puts families under stress?

Clearly, the answer is that it's a systemic problem that's manifested in an individual. You can't separate the individual from their emotions, their emotions from the context, or the immediate context from the social context. It's not a problem of the individual, it's a problem of the culture. It's a cultural manifestation, not simply an individual physiological aberration.

This approach is completely missing in medical practice. We concentrate only on the organ and its particular immediate pathology, rather than looking at the larger context. We're looking at the trees and not the forest. Or not even the tree—just a particular branch or twig or leaf.

What is striking is that we have the science to prove otherwise. The unity of mind and body, the biopsychosocial nature of human beings, and the fact that our biology is shaped by our social and psychological relationships and states, all have been abundantly researched and demonstrated.

From a scientific point of view, that's not even controversial. My critique of my medical ideology, the ideology of the profession in which I was trained and worked for decades, is not that we don't have the science; it's that we fail to apply it. Science has proven what the Buddha said 2,500 years ago, what any system of spiritual exploration has taught for thousands of years—the fundamental unity of everything, that everything is connected to everything else. Science has shown the pathways, clarified the physiology right down to the molecular level—yet in our practice we completely ignore all of that. Never mind that we ignore ancient wisdom—we actually ignore modern science when we practice the way we practice.

Why do we ignore that unity? The fundamental reason is this: the ideology of any major institution in society will always reflect the interests of the dominant group in that society. That includes academia, the media, the educational system, the legal system—and the medical system.

The ruling ideology in this culture is that people are separated, individualistic creatures, hostile and competitive with one another, and that this is our natural state. There are all kinds of reasons why in a capitalist system that would be the ruling idea. Foremost, it justifies the exploitation of people and the disregard for human needs. In ignoring the fundamental interconnectedness of all phenomena, we are just following human nature—or anyway, our false concept of it, a nature of isolation.

The medical system reflects that ideology in its isolation of the parts from one another. It's an unwitting conformity to the dominant ideology of the system. People who challenge it don't get very far in this system. They don't get to high positions. In the education and the training of physicians, people who think this way will not make it high in academia, with rare exceptions. For the most part, it is not where the research funds go.

Another reason we ignore that unity is because to understand the unity of emotions and the impact of social stress I must have some insight into myself; I must have seen how these dynamics have affected me. That means making myself an object of inquiry, which means I have to be open and vulnerable.

The last thing a lot of people who go into medicine want is to be open and vulnerable. In fact, as I can personally attest and have often witnessed, what they want is the authority of the white coat and the stethoscope. They want to be sure and they want to be in charge and they want to control things. They talk about *symptom control*. What a phrase that is!

Medical school is very hard on people. You might look at it as a selection process that weeds out the people who are too vulnerable. You have to put up with a lot of stuff to get through medical school: the long hours, the deference to unreasonable authority, the immersion in a certain jargon, the stress that you are willing to subject yourself to. That promotes the shutting down of vulnerability and selects against the vulnerable. These are the people who become physicians.

Furthermore, in the Western mind, in Western psychology, the best we strive for is to make the ego stronger, to make people more functional. There's no awareness that there's anything to human beings deeper than the ego. But there is a deeper essential self, and separation from it is at the heart of so many of our problems. There is a healing, a wholeness that's available to us, which doesn't occur to the left brain, the Western mind. Physicians have the concepts of cure, but they have no concept of healing.

For example, you might come to me with pneumonia, and if I give you the right antibiotic I can cure the pneumonia. That doesn't mean that you're healed. What I haven't necessarily addressed is *why* you got pneumonia. We think you got pneumonia because you got infected with a certain bacteria. That may be true, but *why* were you susceptible to it?

I believe you succumbed to it because your immune system was weakened. Why was it weakened? Because you were stressed by something. By giving you the right antibiotic we'll cure the disease, but until we look at the source of stress in your life, we can't talk about wholeness, we can't talk about healing in a deeper sense. The real question is: Why this disease? Why in this person? Why now? We have to ask these questions, and answer them.

Very often, the disease not only *has* symptoms but *is* itself a symptom of something deeper that needs to be healed. That's certainly the case with chronic illnesses of all kinds, whether it's ALS or multiple sclerosis or Crohn's disease or colitis or chronic fatigue or fibromyalgia or rheumatoid arthritis—any number of illnesses. These are all diseases that not only have symptoms but are symptoms of some kind of chronic stress that is not being looked at, and of a personality that's separated from its core essence.

Idealistically, I would devise a medical care system or a mental health system that is actually evidence-based. Physicians always talk about evidence-based practice; we keep talking about it, but we never do it. The evidence we look at is narrowly defined and very restricted, completely ignoring the scientific evidence I'm referring to. My point is not that we're evidence-based but that we're *not* evidence-based.

ON THE MYSTERY OF BEING

I don't expect that to change any time soon. As long as the system is materialistic and profit-driven, we're going to resist a point of view that calls for a totally different way of seeing things, and a different set of policies that are not profit-based. As long as research is driven by the profits of pharmaceutical companies, what's going to drive the education of physicians except the profit model of pharmaceutical companies? Most of the articles doctors read were paid for by the people who will profit from those studies.

As long as the needs of this system—and by the system I don't mean the people in the system, I mean the identified needs of the elites who run the system—are determined by profit rather than people, this system is not going to change. I don't have a whole lot of optimism about a rapid change in the system.

In the long term, I believe in human evolution, I believe in human transformation, I believe in the truth manifesting itself in human experience. Ultimately, any system that's based on a misconception cannot last. Ultimately, people are going to find a different way of being and living and organizing their lives and configuring their societies. Ultimately, I'm an optimist. These truths will at some point become the mainstream perspective—even if not any time soon.

How do we create a system that incorporates the achievements of modern civilization while still honoring the essence of human nature, the evolved human needs for contact, connection, and communion? Such a vision is possible and can be achieved as long as we make that our intention—it's possible because it's aligned with our deepest human nature of interconnectedness, what the spiritual teacher and Buddhist monk Thich Nhat Hanh has called inter-being.

Cancer as an Awakening Journey

JOAN TOLLIFSON

Cancer is proving to be an awakening journey, a stripping and grounding process, a waking up to the immediacy of this moment. The location and type of cancer I have (an anal-rectal cancer that invaded my vagina) has sent me on a journey into the bowels of the human experience—precisely the journey I needed. We so often (falsely) measure dignity as being clean and tidy, independent, needing nothing—but I've needed help, and I've been down there grappling with all the things we can't talk about out loud in polite company (poop, pee, bad smells, the body parts that are kept hidden, all those places unfortunately associated with shame).

In the book on aging and dying that I'm working on, I am endeavoring, among other things, to show the hard side of aging, the gritty details that are so often airbrushed out of the picture, and to do this not in a way that invites despair or horror, but in a way that finds beauty in how it actually is. I'm taking a similar approach to writing about this cancer. I'm not mincing words, and some may find it "too intimate," "too personal," or "too graphic," or "too unmentionable," but I am trusting that it will speak to some of you. After all, we're all in this human boat together. We're not *just* a human being. We're not *limited* to the body or encapsulated inside it, and "the body" is not the solid, independent, persisting "thing" we think it is. We are the limitless, awaring presence being and beholding the whole show. But at the same time, we can't *deny* the body or the person. We must all eat and poop, one way or another, however enlightened we may be. And it turns out, this is actually a gift, not a giant mistake.

One of the gifts of apparent limitation, as I've discovered before in other situations, such as losing my right hand early in life, is waking up to the immensity of freedom right here, in exactly this moment, just as it is. One morning during my cancer treatment, for example, I had plans—things I wanted to do. Instead, I had diarrhea, a side effect of the radiation. I had to keep emptying my ostomy bag, again and again. This is a somewhat involved operation, especially doing it with one hand, as I must—it's messy and takes time. As this kept happening, there was a brief second of resistance— "This isn't the morning I had in mind, I don't want this." And then something shifted, and there was the realization, this *is* my morning, this *is* what's happening. And suddenly it was no longer a limitation, a disappointment, a drag, or an unpleasant, smelly task. It was wide open, interesting, perfectly okay, every bit as good as a beach in Hawaii or a trip to the Grand Canyon. (Yes, I really mean that.)

My prognosis is good, but I know that death—when it eventually comes, as it always does—isn't the end. I don't fear it. My death will be the end of Joan, the end of "me" and "my story," my movie of waking life, this particular life-dream, but not of the vastness, the dreaming consciousness, the unbroken wholeness, the Tao—whatever we call this infinite intelligence or awaring presence that has no inside, no outside, no beginning and no end.

Would I have wanted an ostomy? No way. Would I have wanted to go through chemotherapy and radiation? No way. And yet, all of this has had an enjoyable side that I could never have imagined, and I can see that this whole journey of having cancer is an awakening journey, and I'm grateful for all of it. As someone once replied when asked how it was being sick: "It was marvelous!" I concur.

In the same way that I wouldn't have wanted to get cancer, I don't want a nuclear war or another genocide or climate change or a racist-sexist president or factory farming, but I know intuitively that everything that happens cannot be other than exactly how it is. I know that the light and the dark go together like yin and yang, and that somehow, we need the dark to reveal the light. I know that there is something that will still be here even if the whole universe blows up, and that I am that, and that is all there is.

I was surprised after my diagnosis to discover how much I want to be alive. I was returned, more vividly than ever, to the present moment. The astonishing radiance and beauty of every sight and sound and texture is so obvious, whether it is an exquisite flower or a crumpled Kleenex on the table. I'm drinking it all in so deeply. And I am discovering something about love and community and the interconnection of all beings and how important it is to show up for each other. The love and support I've received has been heart-opening and life-changing.

In the hospital, where I was for a few days after my surgery, they rang soft, gentle tinkling bells whenever a new baby was born. I heard those bells at least once while I was there. This living reality is endlessly recycling and evolving, dying and being born, like the waves on the ocean, distinct and yet inseparable, moving together, intermingling, never the same from one instant to the next and yet ever-present as the ocean itself. Whether we call that shoreless ocean consciousness, matter, primordial awareness, boundlessness, unicity, God, intelligence, energy, the Tao, the vibrant dance of existence, the universe, or no name at all, it flows on, ever-changing and yet always here, always now. It is our most intimate reality, obvious and unavoidable, utterly immediate, and yet we cannot know the whole in the way we know information or grasp objects, for it is not outside of us. It is what we are, and all there is. In this unbroken wholeness, there is no inside or outside, no self or other-than-self. Yet each wave, each person, each newborn, each snowflake, each moment is utterly unique and beautiful and precious and unrepeatable and perfectly formed, just as it is.

PART SIX

The Heart of Intimacy

The mystics of all traditions have taught us that love is not to be sought; love is what we are. Love is what is here in each and every moment.

Our relationship is now twelve years old. During the first five years, we were in what we call now with a smile "the nondual honeymoon." Relating was easy, the perfume of romantic love was still very strong, we "knew" ourselves beyond the ego, beyond our individual needs and desires, and we focused on our common dream of building SAND. Intellectually, we knew that the other was not responsible for our wounds, heartache, jealousy, et cetera, but we would soon find out that knowing and being are two different things.

In year six of the relationship, something shifted. Whatever had been holding it together, keeping it peaceful and safe, fell apart. It felt as if the ground had opened beneath us. All the inherited wounds, all the trauma that we had unknowingly carried in our bodies and psyches were coming to the surface. We entered into a journey through dark woods, dancing with archaic fears of abandonment, pain, and raging anger. It was as if all that we had carefully constructed in the previous five years was getting demolished, dismembered, completely destroyed.

It felt confusing, dark, heartbreaking—and yet enlivening. There was nowhere to run and nowhere to hide. We were invited to stand in the crucible of the relationship, to be with all the places in us we had abandoned and rejected. There was a sense of dark luminance cracking us open, and with that a sense of deeper listening and intimacy with ourselves, with each other, and with life itself began to emerge. In this way, we realized that love and intimacy are not based on our needs and expectations.

When we humbly experience our own need to feel safe and we don't project it onto another human being, a deep transformation happens. We can love without demand, without fantasy. The beloved is not here to appreciate and validate our carefully crafted identity, but to challenge and at times disappoint us. Relationships, surely, are the mirror in which we discover ourselves most deeply; they invite us to step into the terrain of the unknown and into the depths of our own hearts.

—Maurizio and Zaya

Reflections on Intimacy

ZHEN DAO

When I was a child, riding my bike, I remember taking note of a bewildering mystery. Whenever I saw a piece of broken glass up ahead, I would naturally alert my senses to avoid it. But just as I drew upon it, my body (not my "self") would suddenly unaccountably jerk the handlebars and turn the wheel directly toward the shard, as if to fulfill my fear—as if to perform some anarchy upon my senses, to say: your prudence is a veil, behind which, incurring pain and wound, is some kind of mystery. You cannot, will not avoid it— however much you steel yourself, with intelligence and foresight, against...life.

Once I was at the beach in North Carolina with a group of friends, college seniors sequestered off-season at a parents' lonely beach house to study for final exams. One evening we were sitting around a bonfire on the beach. I was dreamily watching a spider make its way daintily around the perimeter of the fire. It seemed to be palpating with a kind of probing fascination the exact limits of its heat tolerance, a thin margin around the contours of the logs. Round and round the fire it walked, or rather felt, performing a series of laps as if to exercise its own infernal fascination from the barest border of safety. I'd see it disappear out of sight on one flank, and then, as if I were a familiar waiting to collect it at the train station, I waited expectantly for it to appear again on the other side. There were perhaps twelve of us sitting around the fire; the others were talking or singing desultorily.

Suddenly, as I studied it, the spider leapt a full two feet inward, directly into the heart of the flame. Even before the bright yellow consumed it, its many legs folded inward instantly, as if kneeling. For a blink it was a black grain of sand, before it became smoke. And the flame, unperturbed, flared on. I felt I had witnessed a decision that was closer to desire than suicide. Or that—though I did not have this language at the time—I had witnessed a koan about the existential scandal of care itself. It was this strange sense—the visitation of an insensible absurdity—that made me look desperately to my friends.

At that precise moment, a boy—his name was Tim—looked as desperately at me. I widened my eyes and inclined my head toward him, as if to say, "Did you see?" He nodded, at once gravely and ecstatically, and inclined his head toward me, boring his eyes into mine. He had been watching the spider, too; he'd seen the death leap. We stared at each other, these two children of the world, not quite adults, and the tears streamed down our faces.

At one point in my youth I dropped out of college and tried for a short time to live on the streets of New Orleans. But I was too young to understand that the will to destroy privilege only reinforces it. Finding the willful destruction of my health less honest than the cultivation of it, I took a single dollar and a gift bicycle from a local shop and rode across the country—working for food and begging for shelter—to San Diego, and then up the California coast to Palo Alto, where my brother was in graduate school.

At one point in West Texas it began to pour. I was so lonely that, writing a poem in my mind, I compared the glowing light of a Shell gas station to the palm of an outstretched hand. (Poets will painfully remember their most saccharine lurches.) I wheeled my bike into the convenience store and sat in the corner on the floor.

Many hours later, an old man asked if I needed a place to stay. I said yes. He drove me down dark desert roads to a lonely little house. He said he had only his own bed, but that he'd make room. He must have been past seventy; I was maybe nineteen. Throughout the night he pressed up against me. I moved further and further to the edge of the bed, until I could move no more. There, like some human

ON THE MYSTERY OF BEING

flotsam congealed, abject and truthful, we rested, his erection pressed against my thigh, my back turned to him. I was clothed and strong. He was old, frail, and, I surmised, not completely sane.

In the morning, standing in the kitchen, he took me by the shoulders and said, "San Antonio." He said it over and over again, with increasing emphasis. Something had happened there. Perhaps he had fallen in love there; perhaps someone he'd loved had been killed, shot, or hit by a car; perhaps he'd made love to a young man that looked like me; perhaps he'd been mentally well, and my trust in his hospitality recalled to him his sanity.

"Yes," I said, "San Antonio." He then wept uncontrollably. I held him fast and long. Then he took me back to the Shell station where my bicycle had been safely stored.

Your lovers, whoever they are, are waiting for you to cry. Not because you or they have done anything wrong; not because you are sorry—not only that. Those who love you are waiting for you to cry because you will not become the person you were born to be. Because Jung and the Buddha are wrong. You will not self-actualize, you will not enlighten. And you see that truth reflected only in your loved ones' eyes; that is why they are looking at you so intently. For to conceive an attainment is to lose it. To fulfill a destiny is to close a septillion doors.

Your purpose is not to understand yourself. Your purpose is to hold your beloved's gaze, the gaze that disorients your ambition and destroys your attainment, until the space between you is more real than your selves. If you can exist there, insubstantial but with dignity, prayerful but without purpose, sycophantic neither to birth or death or the afterlife, almost beyond grateful, so that you are nothing so much as awe…then you are life's intimate. The very air will undress your soul. That undressing, in a holier time, we called emotion. Your lovers are waiting for you to cry.

Awakened Relating: Being Awake to Our Infinite Nature in Finite Human Relationships

LYNN MARIE LUMIERE

Nowhere does duality and separation appear more real than in our close relationships. We long to connect, yet in relationship we experience two bodies, two personalities, two sets of conditioning, two different perspectives, and two different sets of preferences. We struggle to find connection and intimacy within all those differences. We search for connection by looking for a personality that resonates with ours, or those who share our points of view, preferences, and interests. This may initially help us to feel more connected, but ultimately it does not satisfy our deepest longing to be united in our shared being.

True intimacy is only found through being awake to our shared being and relating as that, while fully appreciating all our differences. I call this Awakened Relating. This is relating from, and as, the wholeness of our self. Relating only from our conditioned, separate identity obscures our wholeness, and our partner's wholeness. Consciously including the infinite being we share, and welcoming our limited human nature with all its beauty and flaws, creates a new kind of relationship.

We are human beings, but most of us are not fully embodying our humanness and our beingness. It is through connecting with our beingness that we can fully allow our humanness. And, paradoxically, it is through fully allowing our humanness that we can discover our beingness.

In essence, our true nature *is* love. We actually *are* the love we seek from others, so seeking love outside our self takes us farther away from discovering the source of love. And, any resistance to who we are, or who the other is, will also lead to losing touch with the love that is always and already here.

When we fall in love, we are looking into a magical mirror that reflects our essential nature; we are actually falling in love with the beingness we share with all "others." Seeing through the eyes of infinite love, we accept all that our beloved is. And, when we regard another, or ourselves, with unconditional allowing, whatever needs to change transforms naturally.

Living in an imagined separation and being unaware of our shared being is the root cause of our relational challenges, both personally and globally. We must address these challenges at their root or they will not resolve. Relating within separation results in relational wounding. All of us experienced some wounding in our childhood that shapes how we perceive our selves and relationships. Even if we did not have trauma such as abuse, we all had some form of hurt that occurred in relationship as children that manifests in our adult relationships.

The healing of these wounds involves bringing them into the light of conscious awareness and fully allowing them to be experienced. This is the alchemical magic of Awakened Relating—all appearances of separation dissolve or transform in the light of nondual awareness. Relationship is the greatest opportunity for this, because that is where our primal wounds come up to be healed. Yet, without this understanding, we all too often rewound each other rather than heal.

In order to experience Awakened Relating, we must experience our infinite being, even if it is just a glimpse at first. This awakening is not the "pie in the sky," big-deal experience that we may imagine.

One doorway into being that is always available is to simply recognize the awareness that is always present and is looking out of your eyes right now. It is the awareness that is reading these words, while also being aware of your body and the environment you are sitting in, all at once. I am pointing to a simple shift: from being aware of inner or outer objects, to being aware of awareness itself. Then we know the knower—the silent background of presence in all experience. As we get to know this presence more deeply, we discover that it is the only thing we can rely on at all times for everything—wisdom, solutions, love, happiness, comfort, healing—everything.

As we learn to rely on the stable wisdom of our own being, we can turn to that when there is conflict in relationship. The conditioned mind is not a source of wisdom. It only perceives and acts according to what it has been taught. We do not find solutions or resolutions there. The imagined separate self can only push away experience or react to it. It is incapable of being present with what is, especially when its self-image is threatened in relationship. Acceptance of "what is" is what brings true resolution or transformation.

As we get to know the presence of nondual awareness, we have the opportunity to rest as that and allow it to inform what we say and do. The clarity of being can allow projecting or blaming to be seen and resolved within us, so we can respond with love and wisdom rather than reactivity and resistance. The separate ego self cannot do this; we need to tap into the wholeness of our self that includes the infinite self, in order to make Awakened Relating possible. I believe this is our next evolutionary step as human beings.

Relationships cannot be truly harmonious when we relate only from separate self to separate self. Our human race is now evolving to see that the illusion of separation and duality is not working. We need to question the very premises upon which we base our lives, relationships, and institutions. Otherwise, we will be forever chasing solutions that are temporary at best, and highly destructive at worst.

The human race has explored relationship within duality as far as we can take it without threatening our survival. Now is the time to awaken to the truth and unity of our shared being and begin to relate as that. This makes it possible to allow all of our wounded humanness to be fully experienced and transformed, which can then allow our world of division and polarity to be united in peace.

Intimacy and Keeping the Spark Alive

MICHAELA BOEHM

"We get along so well. It's just that the spark is gone."

I have heard countless variations on this theme from couples during my twenty years of couples counseling. Even now, when teaching intimacy workshops, most complaints center around the lack of erotic engagement and the loss of excitement.

The underlying issue is the assumption that a good relationship makes for exciting sexual attraction. In actuality, the very aspects that make a relationship successful can harm your sex life, if you are not aware that sexual attraction and a good, loving relationship require very different, and often opposing, skills and behaviors. Relationship is built on sameness. Sexual excitement is created by difference.

For a relationship to work, the more two people have in common, the better. Common goals, friends, interests, religious and political views, and day-to-day preferences make for a harmonious partnership.

When we first meet someone romantically, everything is fresh. Most of us remember the delicious first weeks of talking into the night, sharing history, opinions, and plans. It feels thrilling to discover common ground and connect deeply. During this phase of enjoyable discovery, the sex feels exciting. The promise of deepening intimacy and the emerging dynamics of the relationship are a potent and enlivening cocktail.

Then, over time, as familiarity grows, the couple develops routines, common friends and activities. By now they've heard each other's best and worst stories, developed in-jokes and shared references. While the newness has worn off, in its place—if all goes well—a harmonious relationship built on commonality sets in.

The relationship now involves the stress of day-to-day upkeep, a business or children. In this process the sexual spark often gradually diminishes...until one day the couple find themselves at home on a Saturday night, in sweatpants on the couch, watching their favorite show, touching affectionately but with no sexual impetus whatsoever. The "spark" has gone.

The important thing to know is that diminished attraction is not the sign of the relationship failing. The lost spark is caused by commonality, familiarity, and too much time spent together without conscious purpose.

Most people, including some couples counselors, try to fix attraction problems with relationship solutions. But this well-meaning strategy is actually counterproductive. Relationship issues are issues of not having enough in common. It could be that values and beliefs are no longer aligning, or the partners want different lifestyles, different preferences around touch, sex, religion, or money; or, most commonly, issues with communication—basically, all the things that in a divorce court fall under "irreconcilable differences." Relationship issues can and should be addressed by a qualified therapist, who can mediate differences in values and contribution and teach communication skills.

Often people worry that when the sexual spark starts to wane in an otherwise healthy partnership, it's a sign of relationship trouble. Diminishing attraction left unattended too long, or not properly understood, can lead to relationship problems, but it's important to know that relating well and keeping the sexual spark alive are different issues with different solutions. This distinction alone has helped many of my clients immensely.

Sexual attraction follows very different principles, which is why we often see couples who have a contentious, explosive relationship but a great, active sex life. While relationship is built on sameness, sexual attraction is based on difference. The stronger the difference and the further apart the two poles, the greater the sexual tension.

So, does this mean that if you have a wonderful relationship you are doomed eventually to boring sex and diminished attraction? The answer is yes and no.

It is not so easy to find someone with whom we can be compatible and have a harmonious, loving relationship, so the relationship aspect should be cultivated and held in high esteem. Reclaiming the spark or, even better, being preventative and keeping the spark alive, is much easier than finding a compatible life partner, because creating erotic excitement is actually a set of mechanics and skills that can be learned. With good information and a bit of discipline, a couple can keep the attraction strong and vibrant throughout the relationship.

With the help of a few simple changes to activities, partners will be able to shift how they relate to each other for the sake of bringing back the spark—or not losing it in the first place. Here are a few suggestions:

Delineate Your Activities

Separate your activities and the different topics of your life and create discipline around keeping them apart. Designate times to discuss money and logistics. Plan dates, travel, and outings that are for romantic engagement only. Decide what activity has what purpose and stick with it. Nothing is less sexy than a discussion about the gas bill during a romantic evening!

Spend Time Apart

Even if you are living together, take some time for yourself. Depending on the demands of your life, this might be anything from just a few minutes to several hours. The important thing is to create an opportunity to come back to yourself and feel who you are. If you have time, pursue your own interests and leave the house by yourself. Pursuing your own interests equips you with new information and new stories to tell.

Recharge with Activities That Bring You Back into Your Body

Before you come together for a romantic occasion, take some time by yourself to step down from the rigors of daily life and reconnect with your body. Take a bath, take a walk, move your body in ways that bring you back to feeling and sensual awareness. Enter the occasion already relaxed and sensually alive and feel how this influences your time together.

Be Considerate and Generous

Come prepared to meet with your partner as your lover, not as a known commodity. Be curious about who they are and give generously of yourself, and your time, energy, and attention.

Stop Touching!

Now, I don't mean you should stop touching altogether, but there is an important distinction between conscious and unconscious touch that many couples overlook. Pay attention to how often you touch your partner in an unconscious way. Consider reducing unconscious touch, as an experiment in building desire. Reclaim this mode of intimacy by making an effort to touch consciously when you want to engage romantically.

Give Each Other Space

When both partners have had busy days, give yourselves some space before you engage. Spend some time apart and don't go into exchanging information, complaining about your day, or discussing logistics immediately. If you are parents, take some time apart after the kids are in bed before you connect again. Separating activities and having breaks to connect with your body between activities is key here.

Date-night Discipline

Most couples' lives are busy enough that they have to schedule time for sex and romance. Be realistic with your scheduling and don't place unfair demands on yourself or your partner. It's unlikely you are going to feel like crazy hot sex right after a demanding day. Focus on each other and try not to talk about topics that have nothing to do with the erotic. Ask each other questions and speak about things you consider sexy. And, for heaven's sake, stay off your phone!

Bringing this practical, grounded awareness to our intimacy allows us to avoid spiritual bypassing and to enter into union through engagement. Brought alive through erotic friction, intimacy can be an eternal dance of bliss, ecstasy, awakening, and love.

The Call of the Earth Goddess: Re-membering a Spirituality of Wholeness

CHAMELI ARDAGH

It was the beginning of time, and the earth goddess, Gaia, was spinning in empty space in an empty universe. She was throbbing with beauty and creative potential.

Uranus, Father Sky, irresistibly attracted to her, desired her so much that he laid himself upon her, inside her, and all around her, making passionate love to her.[1] So surrendered to each other were the celestial lovers that they merged into a splendorous pulsation of pure divine passion. Heaven and earth were one and inseparable.

Out of this divine passion, they gave birth to all the creatures in the universe: the animals, plants, waters, and winds. Everything belonged in their magnificent totality.

However, not all their children were pretty. Some of them were ugly monsters and trolls. Uranus felt so ashamed of these creatures that he tried everything to get rid of them. Each time a monster was born, he pushed them away into the underworld. He hid them out of sight in the basement, without Gaia noticing.

For a while, Uranus lived happily in his imagined world of perfection, but a poisonous fragmentation was brewing at the root of the world.

Eventually, Gaia discovered what Uranus was doing and exploded in anger. "How could you do this to my children?" she

---

1   The myth of Gaia and Uranus is from Greek mythology.

yelled. "How can you even imagine that you could split totality? Pretty or ugly, they're all my children. My love excludes nothing."

Desperate to stop him, Gaia made a plea to her sons to stop Uranus once and for all. Kronos, the god of time, rushed to her aid. Pulling his dagger, he cut off the genitals of Uranus, thus ending the blissful wholeness of his parents' union. In great pain, Uranus escaped up into the heavens, where he thought himself to be safe. He fled away from the hurt and shame, away from the rage of the mother and her untamable nature, hovering far above the earthly mess, where he has been ever since.

This was the moment when spirit and matter became two separate and competing realms in human consciousness, when heaven and earth were split in two. This was the beginning of the dream—or nightmare—of the modern world.

Pledging allegiance to the split-off Uranus, we abandoned our roots in wholeness, in earth and in our own bodies, planting our sense of self in uprooted ideals of superiority, in a rejection of the totality of life. Through Uranus's eyes, we began to see our own bodies and Earth as objects to control and exploit. Our intrinsic belonging was kidnapped by a painful illusion of separation.

Filled with elaborate systems designed to keep us from having to feel the raw power, pain, and ecstasy of our bodies and Mother Earth, even our spirituality began to shape itself in the patterns of Uranus's denial. Instead of guiding us home to union, spiritual concepts and paths became an anesthesia, a way for us to feed into the delusion of control, an escape route from the ache of humanness. Obsessed with transcendence, we chased a freedom further and further away from the unruliness of the great mother, just like Uranus. To this very day, we are feeding the root separation in the name of enlightenment.

At this time in history, the goddess is returning to our spirituality, urging us to descend from our split-off Uranus selves. The path of embodied spirituality initiates us into a freedom unafraid of the dark. We are guided closer to a wilderness of being, to restore our

ON THE MYSTERY OF BEING

capacity to live rooted in wholeness. Millions of women all over the world are gathering in women's circles, holding each other through the gloriously messy process of birthing a new paradigm, for the benefit of all.

Tired of spiritual traditions emphasizing practices and beliefs that reject our bodies, Earth, and all things female, tired of outdated maps of spiritual awakening that tell us the wild realms of our feelings and sexuality are anything less than holy, we ache to embody love in its totality, where there is nothing other than sacred, where we don't need to exile any part of ourselves in order to be free. We ache to embody the unbroken union of Gaia and Uranus that pulsates at the root of this world.

The organic process we call "my body" is pure creative intelligence; we are made of the very same momentum that composts and gives birth, that beats our hearts and balances entire ecosystems in unfathomable perfection. Through the portal of the body, we can hear the voice of a deeper truth, the language of signs and dreams, symbols, poetry, and song.

Gaia herself constantly speaks to us, teaches us, grows us; in the organic and embodied process of opening to her, her wisdom unfolds in us as a becoming. Slowly but surely, we find that our listening stretches deeper and wider; we know how to receive her with senses below the senses, to read the movement of a summer wind through the leaves, to feel the formation of birds in the sky, to drink the smell of wet earth and to know it all to be holy and made of freedom.

Just as a seed doesn't need to be taught how to become a tree, a fruit, or a flower, so your body carries the imprint of how to live rooted in an inherent belonging; how to be a human in a world of diversity, living fully awake to the union that breathes us all.

The Ego Cannot Love

ERIC BARET

We can't talk about love, because it isn't an objective experience. It's what is here every moment—except when I pretend to love or when I want to be loved. When I want to be loved, I want something. When I want something, I don't love. When I no longer want to love or to be loved, when I set myself free from this desire to own or feel something, what is left is love. If there is loyalty to *this* love, it is true loyalty. But every time I love someone, every time I want to be loved, I betray my autonomy—and this betrayal carries a high cost. I cut myself off from my resonance, from true love.

Faithfulness to love isn't something we *do*. It is what is constantly revealed—except when I want to love or be loved. Then there is betrayal, deception—the ego trying to catch something.

Loving someone is a projection, a fantasy—as is not loving someone. Saying that I don't love such or such a person is a fantasy. It's cutting myself off from my resonance. When I say someone isn't friendly, I live in my fantasy, in my arrogance. I am cut off from reality. If I am present, there is nothing that isn't friendly. But if I live in my fantasy, everything that doesn't fit my expectation is unfriendly.

So loving or hating belong to the same fantasy world and have nothing to do with reality. The nature of things is love. Therefore I can't say that I love anything. Loving someone would mean loving others less. That is not love, that is lack of love. Love isn't exclusive, it's inclusive. Some people love their children more than other children. That's pathological. The child in front of me is my child.

Needing love, needing to be loved—we need to set ourselves free from this fantasy from women's magazines!

No one ever loved us, no one will ever love us. No one can love. The ego cannot love. People don't love you; they project onto you the answer to an expectation. When you match this expectation, they love you. When you no longer match it, they throw you away and take someone else to love in their own way. We don't need this kind of love.

Needing to be loved is a disease; so is needing to love. The disease resolves itself in the awakening of somatic sensitivity. When this awakens, we become free of imaginary needs. Need is future. In sensitivity, in the moment, what could I need? The question doesn't mean anything.

To be in love is pathological. Like any emotion, it has moments of total beauty. When you are dead drunk or high as a kite, when you overeat or overexert yourself, you can experience moments of sensory madness—which are also moments of meditation. Being in love also includes these moments, which go beyond our usual functioning.

Being in love is the expression of a lack of love. It means that everything I am not in love with becomes second priority. I am in love. If someone needs me I don't have time for them because I am in love! That is not right. We are in love with what is here now, not with someone we need to go visit, neglecting all the suffering in our immediate environment.

The only true faithfulness is to this obvious fact.

Unconditional love for someone is a teenage girl fantasy. It's unconditional...until it's conditional.

Most human beings need to be in a couple to live in a certain harmony. Many people like to talk and they need someone to listen. Of course they could talk to the wall, but most people have too many concepts to appreciate the depth of the wall. That's why they get married; but it's only a question of time before they talk to the wall.

For most, marriage is a good deal. "If you give me this, I'll give you that. If you love me, I'll love you." That's what most people call love. It's surprisingly unpractical, but it's appropriate for many.

Most people need an image of security. They need to know twenty years in advance whether or not someone will call them "my love."

Physical attraction rarely accompanies intellectual or emotional attraction, but in our artificial and rigid societies we've created structures where you have to find it all in the same person. In every being you meet there is depth, but the ego wants security. So we've created institutions that sanctify the ego's fear. The ego is so scared that it started owning these sacraments religiously, so people respect another's "wife" or "husband." Perversity has pervaded our psyche to such an extent that we respect what doesn't exist: fear, property.

Human beings aren't anyone's property. But the ego needs to pretend, and for that we create chains that people wear on their ring finger. They are proud to be chained. They love one person more than another. This invention is respected by society. The sacraments are bestowed by beings dressed as dark ghosts, who often hide their repressed urges under a religiosity erected as morality.

At one point you no longer relate to these pathological carica-tures. It is normal for some people to be delighted when the football team with the same accent as theirs scores a goal, but the day comes when you no longer feel aligned with this type of behavior. You realize how unhappy someone must be to feel complete when a piece of leather crosses a line, to imagine that they own a man or a woman and believe in a bond other than love.

This doesn't prevent us, for functional or economic reasons, from taking part in the strange rites of our societies. At some point, it simply becomes impossible to find any emotion in them.

PART SEVEN

Exploring the Shadows

Exploring the shadows means becoming intimate with anything we have rejected, felt ashamed of, or have kept in the dark because of old, unresolved wounds or trauma.

We have both been searching for the ultimate reality since we were very young. For many years we were on spiritual paths that invited freedom and transcendence. It was about going beyond the "limited form" and any identification with our thoughts or feelings. We left our countries, our families, our culture, and all that was familiar, in an attempt to run away from a painful past. We found states of peace, spaciousness, and serenity for long periods of time. But, in a classic case of spiritual bypassing, we avoided facing any painful feelings, unresolved wounds, and developmental trauma.

Our shadows color our life and influence those around us. They began to make themselves known to us by wreaking havoc in our relationships. Rupture after rupture, we began to meet and acknowledge our wounds, fears, and illusions. Bringing out the dark side, bit by bit, felt disappointing, messy, unflattering, and at times excruciatingly painful. All that we had kept in the dark began pouring forth. We often found ourselves on our knees, screaming, in tears, with our faces buried in the ground.

This journey of descending into human messiness and vulnerability was, to say the least, a deeply humbling experience. At first, we tried to meet our shadow and "resolve our issues" from an intellectual or psychological perspective, but as we went deeper it became clear that the way forward was to focus on the somatic, which in turn revealed an entire universe of sensations and a whole new way of knowing ourselves.

Facing our shadows, venturing into the dark and unknown inner territories, requires courage and vulnerability. But as the negative forces of trauma are transmuted and we begin to integrate and weave the trapped energy into our being, our bodies become more alive, sensitive, and open. We grow more able to surrender to and experience life without judgment. Being a messy, embodied, weird human being becomes much more attractive than showing up wearing a blissful mask covering an ocean of unexpressed pain. In the end, getting familiar with our shadows brings us home to ourselves, creates a greater capacity for relating, and allows life to move more freely through us. Our shadows illuminate our life and create a greater capacity for freedom. As Rumi says, "Both the shadow and the light are the dance of love."

—Maurizio and Zaya

Developmental Trauma and the Transformation of Anger and Rage

JULIE BROWN YAU

The dual nature of trauma can both potentiate and depotentiate our deepest capacity for knowing our essence. In this light, I view trauma as inherently spiritual at its core, as spirituality is about knowing who we are in essence—our beingness. Spirituality points to our direct experience of what feels sacred to us. Healing trauma, I have found, brings us to an experience of sacredness within us. This can be central for connecting to something larger than our individual self, and for the full resolution of trauma. As we heal trauma, we're softened with the strength of vulnerability, reenergized with the unblocked flow of our life force; our heart opens to love, to knowing we are love, and fear diminishes or dissolves. When trauma is left unattended and unresolved, this interconnected and loving relationship to life is evaded.

Developmental trauma, which this article speaks to, also known as early or attachment trauma, is the result of a variety of experiences. Ongoing misattunement within the child–caretaker relationship is one. This early form of trauma also occurs when the infant or child experiences severe neglect, or physical, sexual, or emotional abuse. It can also be caused by early maternal–fetal distress, intrauterine toxicity, premature birth, traumatic birth, post-birth surgery, and illnesses such as colic.

What is less well known is that developmental trauma can result from what didn't happen or what we didn't receive—holding, nurturance, attunement, loving touch, and mirroring. When these essential development needs aren't met, we experience an undefinable threat. For instance, the intense crying of an infant is a call to alert caregivers to tend to their needs. Being left unattended when in distress can feel life-threatening. Their developing brains are flooded with potentially neurotoxic hormones. In the face of perceived threat, with no loving other to tend to their needs, an infant or child has little choice but to shut down and disconnect from their body and overwhelming emotions—to go *away*.

Dissociation is the body's oldest defense mechanism. Dissociation seems preferable to the perceived threat of alienation, abandonment, and perceived annihilation when essential needs go unmet. To avoid the emotional and physical pain and intolerable emotions of trauma, we may seek solace in our intellect or spiritual realms. The parts of our brain that transmit the visceral feelings that convey emotions may shut down, disabling our ability to feel—the pain *and* the joy. Therapeutic efforts in adulthood to resolve trauma need to remain focused on the removal of these emotional blocks.

Anger is a common feeling for infants or children who feel distressed and whose needs aren't attended to. Anger is a call for reconnection, to draw others back to us so we can feel safe in the warm embrace of a loving other. If a child's needs are repeatedly neglected, over time the threat becomes chronic and anger can turn to rage. That rage may be directed at the caretaker the child is dependent on. The child's fear of this rage adds to their sense of feeling threatened—this is simply too much to bear.

To preserve their personal spirit, the child splits off or represses these feelings, in an attempt to avoid the depth of hopelessness, fear, anger, and rage that is so frightening and intolerable. But this relief is temporary and comes at a huge cost. Trauma results in a split in the unity of self; our sense of wholeness is sacrificed and, if left unaddressed, this can last a lifetime.

Unresolved anger, hidden in the shadows of our psyche—as children and in adulthood—may cause us to lash out at others, creating harm and upset, or may be turned inward and experienced as self-judgment, self-loathing, or self-hatred throughout our life. It

ON THE MYSTERY OF BEING

closes the window on our capacity to feel fully alive, and deeply affects our capacity for intimacy and authenticity. Whether directed outward or toward oneself, anger keeps us in a state of separation and disconnection from the full truth of who we are.

When we live with unresolved anger, our system is primed for danger, making it difficult to discern the intentions of others. We may become defensive even when someone is trying to help. We may feel helpless and powerless, disconnected from our vitality, internal strength, and confidence. We may project our anger onto others, seeing it as *out there* rather than within us. Consciously or unconsciously, we will be subject to its presence and frequently negative influence.

Anger emerges from feelings of fear, helplessness, and powerlessness, from our desires and needs being denied, and from boundary violations. It can become a destructive force that will break through the defenses we've constructed to avoid it if we don't address the underlying cause. Anger, when addressed in a healthy way and integrated, loses its destructive trajectory and returns to a more empowering form of life energy, vitality, self-confidence, and aliveness.

Even though the effects of developmental trauma can be devastating, limiting our life and our capacity for authenticity, it can go unidentified. Many of us who've experienced developmental trauma are unaware that we've been unconsciously affected by its long-term, insidious effects. There's a growing epidemic of individuals suffering from fear, anxiety, insomnia, depression, and a feeling of emptiness, a sense that something is missing, who believe their painful existence, riddled with difficulties and challenges, is just the way life is. This is not so. Often at the root of these uncomfortable states is unresolved developmental trauma.

Trauma separates us from our essence. A common deficit with trauma is the absence of a deep connection to self, as well as to others and the world around us. We feel isolated, numb in our bodies, and disconnected from our emotions; we live in a half-alive state—and are often not even aware of this. When we restore this deep connection, we feel fully alive. As we gather the parts of ourselves that have been split off, rejected, or repressed, it becomes possible to gain access to our essential self. We experience ourselves and our life from a place of deeper self-knowledge, and establish a path to our personal spiritual core, from which we can envision and live a new way of life.

Transformation is gradual and may at first feel tenuous. In the individuals I work with there is an observable fluctuation between feeling like they are falling apart and coming back together. The path of healing is rarely linear, yet with each coming back together another part of themselves is found, tenderly gathered up, and reintegrated. As we leave behind destructive patterns and strategies that were necessary for our survival, the fluctuations settle into a steadily increasing sense of vitality. This can bring a new sense of "coming home" and the courage to continue. Courage and compassion are essential in the process of healing.

As the negative forces of trauma, distorted anger, and rage are transmuted and we integrate and weave the energy into our being, our bodies become animate and we claim our authenticity, inner strength, and wisdom. We learn to recognize, attune, and attend to our own needs, developing a strong sense of personal agency and a vast capacity for all of life's myriad expressions. We step over a threshold into a place that was once frightening territory to traverse alone. Yet with assistance, whether through therapy or other means of support, so much is possible. Resolving trauma returns us to the truth of who we are. You need only begin.

Healing Trauma as a Spiritual Path: Individual and Collective Dimensions

PETER A. LEVINE

From a conversation with Thomas Huebl at the SAND conference,
October 2018.

There are a number of reasons why transforming traumatic experiences opens portals to spiritual experience. And I think it's also important to note: that doesn't mean that transformation is a spiritual path—but it can open to a spiritual path. One reason is because the energies involved with responding to threats are vast.

Think about an impala being chased down by a cheetah on the Serengeti. They're running at sixty-five miles an hour, and in a moment the impala falls to the ground as though it were dead. But it's not dead. This profound activation, this energy, is still revving within the nervous system, within the body, within the organism.

This vast energy is collapsed in the moment that trauma takes over, when we're frozen; we can't open to that energy too quickly, because if we do it's an explosion. I've worked with a number of people who have had premature kundalini awakenings, where the energy was opened too quickly and the nervous system was not able to integrate it. But when we're able to open to this energy a small amount at a time, we can shift these profound energies to those of openness and oneness, of connection, of compassion.

Ultimately, trauma is a disorder of not being able to be in the here and now. Very often people who are attracted to meditation have a lot of trauma in their background. One way of avoiding dealing with trauma is the "bliss bypass." In working with trauma, we must hold together the contraction and the expansion, the light and the darkness. That's one of the gifts that trauma transformed can offer us: we really learn how to hold polarities as a way of experiencing the nonduality of existence. In working this way, at the core of trauma, the person is able to say, "I'm alive. I'm alive and I'm real."

When I was developing my work in the 1970s, I had a profound experience in a restaurant that I used to love to go to. There was the table, my chair, and another chair on the other side—and I felt a presence. I looked up and there was an old man with really crazy hair looking at me. It was Albert Einstein. This wasn't like active imagination, and it wasn't a hallucination either. It felt absolutely real, though I knew, of course, that at some level it came from my inner self.

We had many, many discussions, and one of the questions I asked him was about how trauma pervades societies, from generation to generation.

He took me, via an image, to a small pond. He had a yardstick, and had placed a series of pebbles along the yardstick. He held it over the pond and turned it and, of course, for each pebble there was a wave; the waves overlapped and continued out to infinity. And he said, "That's how the energy is supposed to be transmitted through the generations, from the ancestors." He used exactly those words. "Now," he said, "what happens here where two of the waves overlap? It gets stuck. It's a fixation, and from that point on, everything else is distorted because it's unable to move through." And I said, "Ah! Okay. I get it."

There is a wave pattern, and when you're able to find some of the places where the energy is stuck—he called them "ego points," I call them "fixation" or "trauma points," whether from this or other lifetimes—and open enough of them...then the forward movement of the wave reconstitutes itself and moves on.

This can happen anywhere—with a neighbor, a friend, with someone begging for money on the street. Any place we are able to open just a little bit, the wave continues. It plays out in the inner body, whether in the body of one person or in a collective body.

In doing some work in the Middle East, we wanted to try to find a way to begin to help heal the collective trauma in that region. We worked on a protocol where mothers from both Israel and Palestine would be there with their babies. We used music and rattles—rhythm itself is so important. You could see, at the beginning, the children, awake, alert, looking excited, wanting to take an instrument and make some noise with it. And then you could see the parents connecting with the babies, and the babies connecting with each other, and with the other mothers. This is just one example where you open something and let the ripple do the healing, let the outer movement do the healing. And when any person heals, every time anyone makes this shift, the shift affects everyone. It's a matter of exponential growth.

When I started working in Germany around 1981, nobody would go anywhere near anything having to do with the Holocaust. But when people started to heal—I remember one person whose father was in the SS—that immediately affected another person, whose parents were in the resistance. It's the same trauma. The waves move outward.

Unconscious energy is fixed, like a machine. It is destiny. But when we're able to move from fixity to flow, then it's not destiny, it's informed choice. That's why people meet together in conferences and meetings—to move out of the fixity into the flow, into the reconnection, into new connections. We're opening up one more area of the fixation and allowing the energy to flow. Trauma is about broken connection: to self, to others, and to spirit.

There are patterns as we heal. People who are stuck in the grip of trauma, everywhere they look, every person they meet, they're banging into their trauma. Then as you work on it for a while, you rub up against the trauma and it gets smoother. At first, the trauma is like a sharp piece of wood, but as you learn to move through it the wood becomes more like a round surface. Instead of getting caught on it, you just rub against it and move on.

This is a process of becoming more alive and more embodied, and that's a minimum of a life's work. To transform trauma is easy. For the personality to change, that takes a lifetime.

Mongolian Shamanic Trance

CORINE SOMBRUN

In 2001 I went to Mongolia to do a radio report for the BBC World Service about Mongolian mysteries. I didn't know much about shamanism, but a Mongolian friend of mine, Naraa, accompanied me to the north to meet a shaman and attend a ceremony.

As soon as the shaman started beating his drum I began to tremble and shake, and feel as if I was an animal. I began howling and sniffing like a wolf. I had paws instead of hands, a muzzle instead of a nose. I was completely conscious of what was happening to me, but didn't have any control over it—I was becoming a wolf, and had no way to stop it. I had never had this kind of experience before and thought I was going crazy.

When I came out of this scary state, the shaman and Naraa spoke together, for a long time. Everybody was looking at me, then at him, then at me, then at him; I thought something bad was about to happen. Maybe I had done something wrong. Finally Naraa translated and told me the shaman was not happy because I hadn't told him I was a shaman. The drum's effect on me meant the spirits desired for me to be a shaman. I had received the shamanic spark. He told me I had to stay three years with him to be taught in the shamanic tradition.

The shamanic spark! I didn't want the shamanic spark. I told him, "I don't want to stay three years with you at the border with Siberia. I am a French woman, a Parisian. I like my piano and my computer. I like my life. I don't want to stay three years in the middle of nowhere. No way! It's minus fifty degrees in winter. It's cold."

The shaman replied, "If you don't become what the spirits have decided for you, they are going to be unhappy with you. And if you think your life has been a bit of a mess up to now, it's nothing compared to what your life could become." Then the shaman told me I could come for two or three months a year, so I decided to do it.

It took eight years. To start with I was just a regular Westerner asking questions. I call it my "W" period: What? When? Why? Who? All day I questioned, and for an answer I always got, "The spirits will teach you."

"But how can the spirits teach me anything? I can't see them. What do you mean?"

"The spirits will teach you."

It was so annoying! As a Westerner I was used to asking questions and getting an answer.

After about three years of training I could report objectively about the various effects of trance.

The first effect is timelessness. You lose the feeling of time. It's like when we are absorbed by something we like to do, something we are passionate about. You think fifteen minutes have passed but it was two or three hours.

The second thing is, you don't feel pain, and your strength increases. The big drum is very large and heavy and I hurt myself with it at the beginning. Later I could easily hold it for hours. There was a big increase in strength. This also happens when you are angry. If you are fighting with somebody, you don't feel the pain. After the fight, you feel it. It hurts.

The third effect is a modification of the senses. For example, I no longer smelled odors, but the information behind the odors. I was able to sniff discord. I could be in a place or with people and I could smell a lack of harmony. As soon as I sniffed this discord my body would start making gestures, or speaking languages I didn't know— singing, shouting. The senses were working at a more subtle level. I was not Corine anymore, I was a wolf—though it was not always the same animal. I might be an ant, a snail, or a fly—and I might also be a person. An old man. A woman might possess me and I'd speak or sing as her. It's a zoo, and you don't know what's going to show up.

The fourth thing is visions. You have visions, all around you. You see animals, people, geometric shapes. And the consciousness of self is decreased, so you are not what you used to be. Suddenly you are something you don't know. You sing songs you don't know. You can speak completely unknown languages. You don't know how you're able to make all these sounds, with the full range of the voice, from low to very high notes, which you can't do in the normal state.

The fifth effect is information. In the trance, your brain is able to receive much more information than you are used to having. You can also get this information through intuition. Sometimes when you enter a room, you feel bad. You might feel that something happened there—and you discover there had been an accident. Everybody sometimes feels through intuition that a place is good or bad. It's the same with people you meet. Sometimes we don't feel good about a person. We don't know why, but we don't feel good. That's what you feel during a trance. Suddenly, you are able to smell information—and you know if it's discordant or not. You are making sounds and gestures, and you know that this is happening to improve the situation and make the discordance disappear, to get the harmony back. It's what the shaman calls a "repair."

The goal for the shaman is to ask questions of the spirit and come back with answers. For example—a very simple example— you've lost your keys and want to know where they are. In our tradition, we run around, become hysterical, but don't find the keys. In the shamanic way, we just induce a trance and ask the spirits.

That's the difference between Westerners and this traditional culture. For them, the spirits are helpful. If he's a good shaman and he asks a spirit, he'll get the information. Everything around us is holding information. We don't know how it works, but it works. We don't know how this information enters our brain in this special state. The brain is an interface, capable of processing ten or eleven million bits of information per second, though only sixteen bits get registered consciously. The brain is a filter, making sure that all the information does not enter consciousness.

During my time there, I had two questions. First: Who am I? Clearly I am much more than I thought I was. What I experience in the regular state is just a small part of what Corine could be. So who is Corine?

And the second question was, Why is this happening? How could a drum change my behavior so deeply? I couldn't accept that it was a magical thing. I thought that the sound of the drum was doing something to my brain, was changing my brain functioning, and I wanted to prove it. So I decided to go back to France to meet some scientists and do some EEG tests, to understand what was happening to me during the trance.

Note: *Corine's wish to investigate the mechanism of shamanism scientifically led to the first neurophysiological study of a normal subject capable of inducing a shamanic trance state at will. This was published in* Cogent Psychology *on March 31, 2017 (Flor-Henry, et al.), and suggests a unified psychobiological model for "altered" modes of consciousness, which incorporates objective, subjective, and intersubjective science within a broad evolutionary framework, helping to bridge Western and traditional healing techniques.*

Dreaming the Mystery
of Being Aware

STEPHEN LABERGE

"Nothing happens unless first a dream."

—Carl Sandburg, "Washington Monument by Night"

Every night we enter another world, the world of dreams. While we are dreaming, we usually implicitly believe that we are awake. How is it that dreams seem so convincing that we take them for reality? What exactly are dreams? Where do they come from? And what do they mean?

In the last century, scientists discovered that dreams are associated with the paradoxical stage of REM (Rapid Eye Movement) sleep, which evolved some 140 million years ago. Today any viable theory of dreaming must apply equally to the multitudes of other mammals who have REM sleep and, as we shall see below, presumably also dream and have some form of consciousness.

Whether awake or asleep, the brain constructs a virtual model of reality—the contents of consciousness—from the best available sources of information. Awake, those sources are external sensory input in combination with internal contextual and motivational information. During sleep, little external information is available, so consciousness is constructed from internal sources. These include expectations derived from past experience, motivations, wishes—as Freud observed a century ago—but also fears. The resulting experiences are what we call dreams. In these terms, dreaming is perception free from external sensory constraint, while perception is dreaming constrained by sensory input—hallucinations that happen to be true.

While dreaming, we experience events as if they were actually taking place for us. Freud—and surprisingly many psychiatrists today—thought this was because the critical faculty was abolished during sleep. However, we do not experience the fact that experience is a dream, nor that what appears to be happening in "the outside world" is really happening in the virtual reality of our own dream worlds. Thanks to millions of years of evolution, the correspondence between experiential or "phenomenal" reality and "physical" reality is close enough to safely conflate the two. So, dreaming or awake, we perceive events as if they were simply happening.

However, we do not usually question the nature of reality while awake either. Modern science tells us that what we see around us is the product of our brain's unconscious inferential processes computing a reality. This makes no common sense at all; we just open our eyes and see. We are usually no more aware of the neural mechanisms underlying consciousness than fish are aware of water. In fairness, neuroscientists studying the mechanisms of consciousness don't yet have widely accepted shared theories, in contrast, say, to chemists or physiologists.

However, there are features of consciousness that afford plausible explanations at useful levels of detail. For example, a major function of consciousness is as a kind of multimodal user interface (MUI). According to the user interface model, consciousness functions something like the graphical user interface (GUI) of computers. The GUI allows the user to conveniently get things done by moving "icons" around a virtual desktop, discarding a "document," for example, simply by "dragging" it into the "trash can." The resultant "user illusion" is so convenient, in fact, that the user can simply ignore all the technical mechanisms actually at work within the computer, saving us time and effort.

Similarly, the user illusion of consciousness allows us to interact with an adaptively simplified "dream," rather than an impossibly complex incomprehensible reality. Seeing is believing. Thanks to millions of years of evolution, it works.

One of the major ways in which dreaming differs from waking experience is that dreams are markedly more easily forgotten—so much so that Sigmund Freud misattributed the reason for our repression of them to socially unacceptable dream content. Dreams are difficult to recall upon waking, with most people only remembering them once or twice a week. Yet even people who have rarely remembered a dream are likely to do so if awakened abruptly from rapid eye movement (REM) sleep.

Still, why should dreams be so hard to remember? Evolution is a likely factor, as explicit recall of certain dreams might well have fatal consequences. Suppose someone dreamed that a deadly toadstool was not really poisonous if consumed under the full moon. If the dreamer later remembered this as fact, they wouldn't be likely to live long enough to pass on genes for remembering dreams! Whatever functions dreaming serves, explicit recall is unlikely to be required or desirable.

The ubiquity of dreaming in mammalian species is still controversial. In accordance with traditional anthropocentrism, human students of dreaming going back to Freud presumed that only humans were conscious, or dreamed. Radical behaviorists will claim that neither they nor any other humans have consciousness. Both of these views are held by some researchers today.

Between these two extremes is another perspective: people and animals with bodies and nervous systems that are closely similar as viewed from the outside would most probably appear analogously similar if viewed from the inside—which is to say from the perspective of subjective experience or consciousness. Thus, it seems more likely that children, cats, dogs, whales, and bats all experience something during REM sleep—far more likely than that *they* just twitch, while humans dream. So what do they dream? What else but what it's like to be a child, cat, dog, whale, or bat.

Finally, to say everybody dreams is just the beginning of the story. By cultivating dream recall and memory for intentions, people can learn to be consciously aware that they are dreaming while still soundly sleeping. This "lucid" dreaming holds the promise of a universal virtual reality in which we could vividly (and safely) experience anything imaginable. Thereby, human dreaming might someday transcend the mammalian average, as squeak, bark, and screech are surpassed by human speech.

And where is nonduality in all this?

I'm a metaphor

A little finger pointing

Beyond either/or...

Fifteenth-Century Alchemy and Twenty-First-Century Liberation

PAMELA WILSON

In the fifteenth-century alchemical text *Aurora Consurgens*, the Moon beseeches her consort the Sun: "Turn to me with all your heart. Do not refuse me because I am dark and shadowed." For whether in her dark phase or her radiant fullness, she is ever the same.

All quests are inherently the same—whether for discovery, creativity, wisdom, value, wealth, or eternal life. We are drawn by that which is shiny and reputed to add value, and we turn away from that which seems to tarnish or diminish us. Whether we explore the terrain within or without, we notice distinctions of this and that. The intellect assigns names, meaning, and hierarchy; be it flora or fauna, emotions, forms, or functions, they are added to our maps. The mapmaker does not notice the openness in which everything is taking place.

The mapmaker does add, as the central point of the compass, the viewer, the personal "me." This eternal explorer, aided by a faceted intellect, seeks to make sense of and surmount the clanging collisions of opposites and oppositions, to arrive at peace, the land of plenty and restful constancy.

Early alchemists and sages were passionately curious, studying the stars, nature, and the terrestrial elements, looking for what has unshakable eternal value. The gold they sought was not the sun, not the metal, but the unchanging, the eternal, the constancy that animates the ever-changing. They sought to live the great promise of wisdom, satisfaction, and rest.

So, too, modern sages, with all their unique talents and training, bring fierce attention to what is real. As Ramana Maharshi spoke: "That which is Real is that which never changes." How then to bring balance to the apparently ever-changing mind and emotions? To live this felt sense of being, we think we must liberate the past, the containment, misperceptions, and ancient survival movements within. Thus, the quest is to tame or banish these functions. But this very passion can move against the mind and emotions, further constraining them and frustrating the would-be sage. The plethora of helpful hints from ancient wise ones, and the body-mind, gets tighter and tighter—until we reach the grace of frustration or exhaustion, when even spiritually tried and tested tools malfunction, when opposition itself collapses to its knees.

The value of sitting with a seasoned sage is timeless shortcuts. The old alchemist says, "Don't follow the book! Read within. Be still, listen, notice." H. W. L. Poonja summed up his life's wisdom this way: "Look within. Approach everything with devotion and gratitude. Stay as heart." And Lao Tzu said, "Be like a kindhearted grandparent within." I suggest that Jesus's counsel to turn the other cheek was a faulty translation of "Do not turn away." Turn toward that which is dark and shadowed, though the body may tremble and protest. Be still. Stretch out as substratum.

The body is the alchemist's crucible. Warmth is that which liberates the body. Apply the warmth of compassion and kindness and the body opens, clarifies the past, and rests into its original relaxed, rooted strength and spaciousness.

How curious it is that the alchemists and sages pursued distilling to extract the essential nature, as do vintners for fortified wine! Meditation does the same thing. So does inquiry. "Who am I?" "To whom does this thought come?" Inquiry into any field or art results in gold.

The sage-alchemist suggests we warm the crucible of the cranium with respect, give a deep inner bow to the galaxy of intelligence and service that is the mind, stay with that timelessly, and watch this galaxy being unbound, stretching into the space around the head, all opposites reunited, dissolved, and resolved in stillness.

In the absence of opposition, and in the presence of respect, the vibratory rate of love and life is uncontained, relaxed, and stunning, warmly reconciling all opposites in the alchemical wedding. Neither this nor that, neither free nor bound, neither spiritual nor unspiritual. No longer human or divine. Neither subject nor sovereign.

And the body-mind, life's own, remains aloft and at rest, distilled to its essence of silence and intelligence, open, soaring, and aware. Golden presence, fortified essence, occasionally intoxicating!

Reconnecting to a Child Within

EDWARD FRENKEL

Adapted from a conversation with Adyashanti at the SAND conference,
October 2017.

I was asked to contribute a chapter to a book about artificial intelligence (AI) safety. It's a very serious book for researchers and computer scientists, published by an academic publisher. AI safety is an important branch of computer science, addressing how we can write programs so that robots don't turn against us, so to speak. The editor asked me to write about what I call the first person perspective, so I shared a personal story about how I came to turning the gaze inside.

What led me to it was a child inside me. There was a voice that had always been there, but I had refused to listen to it for a long time. There were experiences in my life, in my childhood, of which I was not fully aware, and a wounded child longing for my attention, for my love, who wanted to be held and nurtured. It took me thirty years to finally hear his voice, and it came as a shock! My first question was: How could I not know about this? Why didn't anybody tell me? Of course, later I realized that maybe they did tell me, but I wasn't willing to listen yet. I spoke about this in detail at the SAND Conference in 2014.

I see now that there were parts of me from which I was disconnected; I had not yet met them. There were events in my life that were very painful, and as a child I was not yet equipped to handle that kind of pain, to accept what was happening. This created what psychologists call "dissociation." A splitting. That child was frozen inside me and my connection to him was severed.

But the child wanted to come out. At every opportunity, he wanted to let himself be known to the adult. But it's a catch 22. You might ask, "Why didn't you connect with him?" However, to connect, you have to take that pain that was rejected in the first place, and the conscious mind says, "I don't want this pain." Who wants to experience pain? Yet if I don't connect, my life is incomplete. There is no wholeness. Life cannot be fully experienced.

I had several boys inside me, who had been neglected. When I realized that, I felt so ashamed that I had left them for so many years on the battlefield of life, like fallen soldiers. And they were just waiting for me... It's almost as if I left the little ones there to fight the battle, to fight adversity. And they said to me, "Edward, there's only one horse, and you have to get on that horse and gallop away to safety. But come back when you get stronger. Come back and rescue us."

When I finally met the boy who was frozen, it felt like finding a dead boy. That's what I felt, that he was dead—and this was an incredibly sad moment. You grieve for this lost child. At first, the pain can just feel unbearable, even to an adult. But what I found is that if you don't turn away, if you take him and hug him and give him your warmth, then he will come back. And this is absolutely stunning! Literally, you bring somebody back from the dead. He is like Lazarus.... He came back and he wanted to tell his story.

There is an argument that is often made in the nondual community, that all this was in the past and therefore it doesn't exist. Look, they say, the past is just an idea that we have in the present moment. There is no such thing as the past—there are only memories of the past—so there is no need to "go there," because it's not there.

But those difficult moments in which we did not accept what was happening—we carry these moments with us *in the now*. They are not in the past! These moments were always with me. That boy was always with me, because I never accepted what had happened to him, I never allowed that experience to move through me.

Even though these children inside ourselves are frozen, their presence affects us at every moment. They block us from going further. Before I was able to connect with them, I had all sorts of ideas about reality—standard stuff that you read on the science websites. These kids had been holding the door closed, as if to say to me, "Attend to our needs first. Give us love, give us warmth, resurrect us. Only then, through us, will you be able to connect with those parts of reality that have been hidden from you."

Because I had severed my connections to those little boys, I could not experience the world through the eyes of a child. I had lost the capacity to be vulnerable, to be spontaneous, to be authentic— I'd lost the innocence of a child. Carl Jung spoke in very poetic terms about the archetype of the divine child, what it represents to all of us. But if I am not aware of my own very concrete, wounded child, I lose this archetypal connection, and at least some of the dimensions of the heart are closed to me.

It was only after I was able to connect with at least some of those experiences, only after those little ones emerged from the land of the dead into the land of the living, that I was able to see those other dimensions. It's as if these kids opened the door and said, "Look, Edward!"

One of the things I saw was how naive and, frankly, vapid all my ideas about evolution, consciousness, reality, and so on were. I saw that those were just stories spun by my frightened ego as a way to avoid facing reality, to avoid finding out who I am.

I wrote the article for AI researchers. The editor asked me, "What are your practical suggestions?" I said, first of all, our science programs, especially computer science programs should include courses in psychology. The concept of dissociation should be presented. Now, I have no illusions about this; someone who is not willing to listen will find a way to avoid it. But there might be someone who *is* ready, and that's how a connection could be made. And second, we scientists should take matters into our own hands and talk about our personal experiences. We should put some time aside when we meet, and share these experiences. Our stories have so many common elements. When one of us speaks, others will follow.

PART EIGHT

Doorways to Heaven

Western culture is heavily biased toward safety and functionality. We seek comfort and pleasure, and we deny or bypass experiences that do not fit into our rosy picture of the world. This prejudice extends all the way to our spiritual quest, creating unrealistic expectations that the pain of our human experience will disappear once we awaken. But that isn't the nature of life, and it's not the nature of awakening.

There are no easy answers to our soul's deepest yearnings. Any spiritual journey inevitably includes the "dark nights of the soul," the agonizing experience of being taken apart, the utter destruction of who we thought we were and what we believed we knew, the painful process of metamorphosis and attunement.

On the path, many of us have found an opening to God, to reality, to ourselves, through one or many life-changing events, through a privileged experience, through a portal that allowed for a new recognition of our true nature, an initiation into existence beyond control, and a taste of true surrender. For us, sitting with a loved one departing from this world, being with the grief of losing a beloved, facing a near-death experience, meeting death in all its expressions—these have always been guides into the mystery.

Other pivotal gateways in our own journey included psychedelics and spontaneous kundalini experiences. These gateways brought us to complete annihilation of the separate self, giving us a taste of absolute unity with all. These experiences, which illuminate through darkness, have been described by mystics and poets of all times. They cannot be purposely sought, for their very nature is fleeting. They come to us through grace, to shine light on the source while infusing and inspiring our daily life.

In this intelligent and reflective universe, each moment, every experience holds the key to knowing ourselves more deeply. Grief, sadness, joy, disappointment, desire—all the forms through which the divine appears—are the medicine we need to absorb in order to truly taste our essence. Only in that surrender do we no longer limit the mystery of love's expression, and clearly see that love is never not here.

—Maurizio and Zaya

The Science and Mystery of Consciousness

PIM VAN LOMMEL

According to our current medical concepts, it is not possible to experience consciousness during a cardiac arrest, when circulation and breathing have ceased. But during the period of unconsciousness due to a life-threatening crisis like cardiac arrest or coma, patients may report the paradoxical occurrence of enhanced consciousness—experienced in a dimension without our conventional concept of time and space, but with cognitive functions, with emotions, with self-identity, with memories from early childhood, and sometimes with (non-sensory) perception out of and above their lifeless body.

In our prospective and longitudinal Dutch study on near-death experience (NDE) in 344 survivors of cardiac arrest, published in *The Lancet* in 2001, it was found that there were no physiological (lack of oxygen of the brain), psychological (fear of death), pharmacological (given medication) or demographic factors (religion) that could explain the cause and content of an NDE. We studied patients who survived cardiac arrest, because this is a well-described life-threatening medical situation, also called clinical death.

The definition of clinical death we used was the period of unconsciousness caused by lack of oxygen in the brain, due to the arrest of circulation and breathing that happens during cardiac arrest in patients with an acute myocardial infarction. These patients will ultimately die from irreversible damage to the brain if cardio-pulmonary resuscitation (CPR) is not initiated within five to ten minutes.

This is the closest model we have of the process of dying. Through many studies of induced cardiac arrest in both human and animal models, cerebral function has been shown to be severely compromised during cardiac arrest, with complete cessation of cerebral flow. Electrical activity, in both the cerebral cortex (EEG) in human patients and in the deeper structures of the brain in animals, has been shown to be absent after a very short period of time (ten to twenty seconds). The lack of oxygen causes the loss of consciousness, of breathing (apnoea), of all body reflexes (cortex), and also loss of all brainstem reflexes, like the gag reflex, the corneal reflex, and fixed and dilated pupils.

In four prospective studies with a total of 562 survivors of cardiac arrest, between 11 percent and 18 percent of the patients reported an NDE. In an acute myocardial infarction, the duration of cardiac arrest is always longer than twenty seconds, so all survivors of cardiac arrest in the four prospective studies must have had a flat-line EEG. Based on these studies, we have to conclude that in cardiac arrest an NDE is experienced during a transient loss of all functions of the cortex and of the brainstem.

Some universal elements that can be experienced during an NDE, like an out-of-body experience with veridical perceptions, or a meeting with deceased loved ones, have important implications for our understanding of how consciousness and memories could be experienced outside the body with a temporarily non-functioning brain. The paradoxical occurrence of heightened, lucid awareness and logical thought processes during a period of impaired cerebral perfusion raises perplexing questions for our current understanding of consciousness and its relation to brain function. A clear sensorium and complex perceptual processes during a period of apparent clinical death challenge the concept that consciousness is localized exclusively in the brain. Patients who are clinically dead would be expected to have no subjective experience at all. Scientific study of NDE pushes us to the limits of our medical and neurophysiologic ideas about the range of human consciousness and mind-brain relation.

With lack of evidence for any other theories for NDE, the concept thus far assumed but never scientifically proven—that consciousness and memories are produced by large groups of neurons and are localized in the brain—should be discussed, because it is not possible to reduce consciousness to neural processes as conceived by contemporary neuroscience. The current materialistic view held by most physicians, philosophers, and psychologists of the relationship between the brain and consciousness is too restricted for a proper understanding of this phenomenon.

Based on this NDE research, there are good reasons to assume that our consciousness does not always coincide with the functioning of our brain: enhanced or nonlocal consciousness can sometimes be experienced separately from the body. An NDE might be considered a changing state of consciousness, based on the theory of continuity of consciousness, in which memories, identity, and cognition, with emotion, function independently from the unconscious body, and retain the possibility of perception.

Since the publication of these four prospective studies on NDE in survivors of cardiac arrest, the phenomenon of the NDE can no longer be scientifically ignored. By making a scientific case for consciousness as a nonlocal and thus ubiquitous phenomenon, this view can contribute to new ideas about the relationship between consciousness and the brain. We should also question a purely materialist paradigm in science.

I have come to the inevitable conclusion that, most likely, the brain has a facilitating rather than a producing function in the experience of consciousness. It is also evident that this conclusion is important for our concepts of life and death, because of the almost unavoidable conclusion that at the time of physical death, consciousness will continue to be experienced in another dimension, in which all past, present, and future is enclosed.

Research on NDE seems to be a source of new insights into the possibility of a continuity of our consciousness after physical death, because it has indeed been scientifically proven that during NDE enhanced consciousness is experienced independently of a functioning brain. We have a body and we are conscious. Without a body we still can have conscious experiences, we are still conscious beings.

I believe now that death, like birth, may be a mere passing from one state of consciousness into another. Based on scientific research on NDE, I cannot avoid the conclusion that endless consciousness has existed and always will exist independently of the body. There is no beginning, nor will there ever be an end to our consciousness. Consciousness seems to be our essence, and once we leave our body, leave our physical world, we exist as pure consciousness, beyond time and space, and we are enfolded in pure, unconditional love.

This new insight, based on NDE research, helps us better understand the mystery of human consciousness.

Grief

UNMANI

In some traditions, those who are grieving are not only given the space to grieve in whatever way necessary—they are also revered, because it is understood that in their grief a doorway between life and death is open. Grief can certainly be a doorway to awakening and a heart-opening embodiment of previously more abstract realizations. As much as loss is terribly painful and heartbreaking, it also comes with many beautiful gifts that can dramatically and irrevocably change you.

I know this from personal experience. Recently, my love, my husband and father of my two-year old son, died suddenly from a heart attack. This has taken me on a journey that has opened my heart in a way I could never have imagined—though I would never have wanted or asked for what has ripped me apart and turned me inside out.

We usually go through life knowing that one day we and everyone we love will die, but somehow we still live in the comfortable bubble of dreaming that it will all go on forever. We take things for granted and filter our experience through the thinking mind, which has the tendency to cloud our pure vision. Death is a slap-in-the-face wake-up call to the reality of life. It is an invitation to live fully in whatever you are doing, feeling, or being, right now. When someone close to you dies—or if you are dying—you have no choice but to face the reality of death. Your dreams have been ripped away. There is no escape from the truth. It can be excruciatingly painful, but also an invitation to wake up and feel what is here now. You can no longer intellectualize or theorize. You can no longer dream of "one day." You can no longer assume "that sort of thing won't happen to me." Here it is, happening right now.

In our society, death is usually hidden away as if it is not very real, so when it does hit you it can feel like a betrayal. We are taught to believe in happily-ever-after dreams, so when death rips your dreams away you are left bereft and without much support or acceptance from people around you. You are then supposed to grieve quietly and sensibly, at the funeral or behind closed doors. You should shed a few tears, and then get over it.

In my experience, the reality of grief is a wild roller-coaster of all kinds of surprising experiences, emotions, and states. Like love, grief can't be negotiated or contained—it takes you on its wild ride whether you like it or not. If you think that you are in control, or that you know how things are or should be, grief will bring you to your knees, show you humility and absolute respect for life. There can be overflowing tears, numbness, wild rage, and insanity in every shape or form. The mind tries desperately to understand what is going on, and fails. There are times of peace and joy—then, just when you think that the worst is over, another wave knocks you to your knees again. The waves of destruction of everything you have believed in go on and on, and you never really get over it. Even if you have already awakened to your true nature, there is no escape from this wild ride. You live the paradox of knowing that ultimately there is never any real separation, and yet there is still the human experience of heart-wrenching separation.

When someone dies, this paradox of separation and no separation becomes even more apparent. The usual boundary between life and death feels porous. We feel the presence of our loved ones, see signs and messages from them. They visit us in dreams or visions. There are times when I feel I slip beyond the veil of death and know that, when the time comes for my own death, it will not be very different from this present moment. Knowing that I am really love itself and that nothing can ever be lost, I know in the deepest way that my husband has not gone anywhere. He was never limited to his body even when he was alive. His body died, but love doesn't die.

In grief, love is set free and often felt even more potently than before. Yet there are many opportunities to fall asleep again—believing, for example, that you are a special "victim," or blaming yourself, or believing that life is no longer worth living. Although all of these are certainly valid aspects of grief, and should not be denied, if you wallow in them endlessly they call you to overlook reality once again. Feel the waves of grief in all its forms for as long as you need to, but don't build a cozy nest in it. Surrender to the mystery of love as it destroys you. This destruction is the only way to make space for the fresh and new.

If you love, it is inevitable that you grieve. There is no way around it. Grief is the other side of love. When you take someone into your heart, you feel them, know their vulnerability and courage. To watch them die is nothing less than having your heart physically torn open. After that, your heart goes on bleeding and you feel the grief of all those who have lost love ones or who are suffering in any way. You are not special or alone in your grief. The nature of life is to love and to lose, and there is no way around that. It is intensely heartbreaking. Yet it is also a heart-opening, humbling and awakening.

Three Basic Freedoms

JAMES FADIMAN

"I regard consciousness as fundamental. I regard matter as derivative from consciousness. We cannot get behind consciousness. Everything that we talk about, everything that we regard as existing, postulates consciousness."

—Max Planck (1858–1947), Nobel Prize–winning
German physicist and father of quantum theory

When I was learning to help others have safe and sacred psychedelic experiences, the substances (LSD, mescaline, psilocybin) came from their manufacturers, and the government freely granted "experimental drug" exemptions to individuals and institutions using it with human subjects. During the years just before the government stopped the program, LSD was the most researched psychiatric drug on the planet. The legal restrictions that were then imposed never had anything to do with science, or even safety. We guessed that then, and we know it now.[1]

When the government shut us down, initially I felt the personal loss of my potential career, as well as disappointment at no longer being able to give high-dose psychedelic sessions. That I could no longer support the chance for people to experience total transcendence in a safe, supportive setting felt deeply wrong.

---

1 "You want to know what this was really all about? The Nixon campaign in 1968, and the Nixon White House after that, had two enemies: the antiwar left and black people... Did we know we were lying about the drugs? Of course we did." —John Ehrlichman, Watergate co-conspirator

It took me a long time to realize that what the government had done was far more corrosive—by restricting the use of the best tool we knew to map consciousness, it had taken away something far more valuable then a breakthrough psychotherapeutic intervention.

I came to understand that certain freedoms are a necessity if human beings are to continue their own evolution. Any restriction of those freedoms, whether by rule of law, religious orthodoxy, or any other reason, prevents that culture's own growth and development. As examples, we can point to the closing of the Eleusinian mysteries in Greece in the fourth century, the Catholic Church's repression of indigenous practices in Mexico and South America in the sixteenth century, or the United States government's restrictions in the 1960s.

The first and most fundamental freedom is the freedom to explore one's own inner being, independent of class, occupation, education, sexual identity, or anything. What we know now is that the poorly named "default network," better called the "defense of self network" (thanks to Mahesh Subrahmanyam for this), maintains enough of the illusion of separation that we can function on the physical plane. In functioning, however, it blocks awareness of the underlying unity and the joy that is also present. Like every other system, it is useful for what it is useful for, but deleterious beyond that. Psychedelics are among the easiest and most widely used tools ever discovered that allow us to slip past the defense network's limitations to rediscover the vast reaches of awareness that exist beyond the boundary of personal separation.

When consciousness is restricted only to this network, individuals come to believe in their separation so strongly that they will hurt others, harm animals, and even destroy their own ecological habitat without recognizing that doing so is a partial destruction of themselves.

Making such exploration illegal comes at a terrible cost.

The second basic freedom is equally basic—the freedom to explore the diversity of the external world, the myriad different species, from the largest whale to the smallest virus; to be able to dive into even the whirling molecules themselves. We have an innate right to discover everything we can about our natural world. Psychedelics allow us to grasp whole systems more easily, as well as to penetrate below the surface of matter to perceive energy itself. As focusing tools, they are the telescopes and microscopes that expand our capacity for discovery. It is no longer a surprise to recognize how many discoveries, inventions, and industries rest on insights first glimpsed on psychedelics. Most of us know about the Nobel prizes linked to psychedelics and the Apple computer, but often forgotten is that it was LSD's resemblance to serotonin that opened up the whole world of neurochemistry and our understanding of brain functions. Making such exploration illegal cripples scientific progress and prevents further discoveries.

To circumscribe their use is as folly-driven as those gentlemen who refused to look in Galileo's telescope because it would force them to let go of false premises and expand their worldview.

The third basic freedom is that every individual should be freely able to explore and discover divinity, in whatever form it manifests. To restrict this most fundamental religious liberty—the right to know God—is cruel and shortsighted. Take away tools for discovery and you take away the capacity to live fully. Imagine a culture that prevented people from learning to read, from learning to dance or to sing. Sadly, we do not have to imagine a culture where an equally basic way of apprehending the unity behind the multiplicity of things has been made illegal. It should never be a crime to open a path to uncovering within one's being that Atman is Brahman, that you and God are one, that Christ-ness is in everyone (and that stones can sing).

It weakens civilization when we make any path to personal revelation illegal. Today, the denial of unity and divinity seems, in part, to maintain those institutions abetting rapid climate change and potential species destruction. Not being able to know who you really are—and who everyone else is and what everything else is—comes at a terrible cost.

ON THE MYSTERY OF BEING

While I appreciate the current "renaissance" of psychedelic research, we have not yet overturned these restrictions on our most basic freedoms. If we do not do so in the near future, it may be too late.

The planet will do fine without us, but I would rather restore the right to use these tools wisely and well, so we might continue to improve not only the well-being of humanity, but of the planet itself.

The Blessings of Brokenness

VERA DE CHALAMBERT

The world's great wisdom traditions celebrate the blessings of brokenness. Consistently, in spiritual mythology, the divine exposes its brokenness to us. And over and over we are invited to step away from our grandiose images of enlightenment and simply accept the holiness of our holy mess. Brokenness is not *in* the way, it *is* the way.

"Where there is ruin there is hope for a treasure," the Sufi poet Rumi reminds us. This is an encouraging way of seeing things as we struggle to integrate the deep challenges emerging in these Anthropocene times. Never has it been more important to embrace brokenness and let it become our ally in our healing process and the healing of the world. Paradoxically, it is our relationship with the broken that determines our intimacy with the real. Like Rumi, we must readjust our expectations. Our brokenness is not a mistake, but an invitation to give up on our projects of fixing ourselves—fixing reality—and to surrender to life. It is so exhausting to keep running from our brokenness and imperfection. What if we stopped running and leaned in for a kiss?

The great Hasidic master Rabbi Menachem Mendel of Kotsk famously said, "There is nothing so whole as a broken heart," echoing the fascination with brokenness pervasive throughout Jewish history, scripture, and mystical tradition. From the permanent dislocation of Jacob's hip while wrestling with the Angel and the broken tablets of Moses at Sinai, to the destructions of the Holy Temple in Jerusalem and the pangs of historical exiles, brokenness can be seen as the central theme of Jewish spiritual life.

At the heart of the Kabbalistic tradition, we find the origin story of the shattering of the vessels. It is said that God first created the world by attempting to emanate into ten holy vessels, ten spheres, or *sephirot*. But something went wrong. God was too eager and poured too much divine light into the vessels. The vessels were unable to contain this immensity of immanence and shattered. God had to start creation all over again, and the purpose of this second creation, our world, becomes Tikkun Olam, or "mending the world." We are meant to do this through gathering the broken shards of the first vessels, by performing good deeds. It is said that each soul comes here to find the broken piece that only it can restore. Traditional interpretations regard the shattering of the vessels as a cosmic catastrophe—but what if it wasn't a mistake, but the actual path? God wants us to know His broken, imperfect nature! After all, the only way to restore the world is in relationship with divine brokenness. The process of shattering can also be seen as a model for our own spiritual lives. To awaken, to be whole, to become holy, we too must first become intimate with brokenness.

The Christian tradition has a particularly eloquent relationship with divine brokenness, through the central theological theme of the crucifixion. Perhaps the most spiritually striking and paradoxical moment in the Christian narrative comes when, after resurrection, Christ remains physically broken. Far from the perfect form expected from a divinely resurrected being, Christ returns with the gaping wounds of crucifixion. Why? Why not a perfectly healed form?

But the story gets even stranger. When Thomas meets the resurrected Christ and asks him, "Master, how do I know it is really you?" Christ outrageously invites him to put his fingers into his wounds, as if to say, if you want to know me, the wound is the way. God's wounds are a reminder to include the broken and irreconcilable in our projects of healing and awakening. Christ's invitation to Thomas is love's commandment to us all. We must embrace our brokenness, give up the idealized images of spiritual perfection, and baptize our souls in the wounds of incarnation. The mystical monk Father Thomas Keating, founder of Centering Prayer, once said, "The acceptance of our wounds is not only the beginning of the spiritual journey, but the journey itself." It is by making contact with our own wounds and the wounds of the world—the most powerless, most wretched, most irredeemable—that we can come to know divine love directly, and embody a spiritually mature, truly nondual faith.

The Hindu pantheon is brimming with divine feminine archetypes that invoke the broken. But the Supreme Goddess Akilandeswari—whose name, from the Sanskrit *akil*, means "complete" or "total," yet who is paradoxically known as the goddess who is "never-not-broken"—is perhaps most relevant to modern spiritual culture hooked on bliss and bypass. Instead, Akila commands, "When things fall apart, don't fix it!" Imperfection, vulnerability, and change are her boons, brokenness is her shakti. An oracle of the groundless nature of reality, she always has her feet in the moving river of life, and is portrayed riding a crocodile, teaching us to face fully our reptilian fears of dislocation, annihilation, and change. Akilandeswari models for us true surrender, yielding to the destruction of her ego so that she can remain intimate with the unruined. Through including radical brokenness in her supreme wholeness, Akila is a truly nondual devi. It is in being fully broken that she can remain the undivided supreme goddess of the universe.

Arising out of Zen Buddhism, an aesthetic philosophy called *wabi-sabi* deeply honors the beauty of brokenness, acknowledging that everything is impermanent, imperfect, and incomplete. Its most popular example is a broken cup whose cracks have been filled with gold, making it an object of value and sacred beauty. The first noble truth of Buddhism is *dukkha*: Suffering is inevitable. Like the cup, we will all break. It is the first condition one has to accept in order to embark on the path of awakening. At its core, this truth is full of tenderness—because life's imperfection isn't a problem, it's reality. Spiritual work is about seeing and accepting life as it is, in its brokenness, its imperfection. Because life is not only suffering, life is *everything*. And suffering, imperfection, and brokenness are not obstacles to true happiness, healing, or awakening, they are the windows. Echoing Rumi, Buddhist nun Pema Chodron says, "Only to the degree that we expose ourselves over and over again to annihilation can that which is indestructible within us be found."

Traditionally, the weeping Buddha is associated with the story of the Buddha accidentally killing his own son in battle. Touching his back, it is said, will take away your sorrow when things fall apart for you, too. Yet the weeping Buddha is no magical amulet to bypass our suffering. It invites our own hearts to break for all beings, to let brokenness be our ally toward tenderheartedness, kindness, and service. The Buddhist Perfection of Wisdom Sutra, from which the notion of the bodhisattva comes, offers a game-changing teaching of interdependent co-arising, which states that awakened consciousness does not in fact merge into perfect bliss, but instead chooses to remain in the brokenness of reality, in solidarity and relatedness with all beings. We belong to each other, and awaken together. The weeping Buddha is a reminder of the limitations of the human condition, of our brokenness and our connectedness.

Divine brokenness pervades the spiritual traditions, and the divine neither hides its brokenness nor turns away from ours. Instead, we are encouraged to pivot fully toward it and let it transform us. If we accept the blessing of brokenness, it will awaken in us the tenderness that changes everything. We might still find ourselves among the ruins, but we will become the treasure.

The Portal of a Poem

MIRABAI STARR

At the end of her brief and startling poem "Eye Mask," Denise Levertov invites us to linger in the wilderness of not knowing, the same terrain to which the mystics of every spiritual tradition point. "I must still grow in the dark like a root," she writes, "not ready, not ready at all."

I'm not ready, either.

Nor is John of the Cross ready, as he so eloquently admits in his mystical masterpiece "Dark Night of the Soul." The Spanish monk has little patience for theology. He does not thirst for easy answers to his soul's deepest yearning. All he is interested in is a secret rendezvous with the beloved in the garden, which he attains by slipping out of his sleeping house in the middle of the night and walking through the darkness, with "no other light, no other guide, than the one burning in my heart."

Classical Indian poet Kabir shows us that he isn't ready when he praises the unknowability of God and says that we can never know the holy one until we *become* that. Contemporary American poet Marie Howe also isn't ready. She composes a verbal sketch of the light that flooded the space where a young Jewish peasant received the Annunciation and, in the voice of Mary, declares that the only way she could endure that radiance was "by being no one, and so completely myself I thought I'd die from being loved like that."

The mystic poets—across the spiritual landscape and throughout time—give thanks for the holy darkness, for liminal spaces. They are at home with ambiguity; they thrive on vulnerability. They eschew dogma and they light belief systems on fire. As soon as the fragrance of the beloved crystalizes into a definition of ultimate reality, they watch the holy one wither and die, and their hearts break. They move away; they move on, seeking sunyata, the vast emptiness that is unutterable plenitude. "The Tao that can be told is not the eternal Tao," Lao Tzu proclaims in the very opening line of the Tao Te Ching. Meister Eckhart begged God to free him from God, and Angelus Silesius pointed out that "God, whose love and joy are present everywhere, can't come visit you unless you aren't there."

My own namesake, the bhakti poet Mirabai, offers herself to Krishna, lord of love, and invites us to join her in being consumed and subsumed, transfigured and recalibrated by the divine. "The single lotus will swallow you whole," she warns us. She is serious, but she is laughing. Sufis call this holy fire *fana*, the annihilation of the separate self, and from Rumi to Rabia they celebrate burning as a path to union. "The grapes of my body can only become wine after the winemaker tramples me," Rumi says. And Hafiz urges us not to "surrender our loneliness too quickly," so that it might fully season our souls. In "The Holy Longing" Goethe concludes that "so long as you haven't experienced this, to die and so to grow, you are only a troubled guest on the dark earth."

For the most part, a good poet is a master of nondual consciousness. Even as she celebrates the particularities of the incarnational experience—illuminating the details of life in a body—she is drawing us into the realm where dualities dissolve and the illusion of separation gives way to the truth of not-twoness. Any good poem, in my view, is a mystical poem, even if it never mentions God by name. The poetry of the mystics does not simply describe God-consciousness; it *evokes* it. Mystical poetry does more than worship the holy in the temple of language; it *invokes* it. This process of evoking and invoking the sacred is the special domain of the poet-mystics. They build an ark of words and the Shekinah—the indwelling feminine presence hidden at the heart of Judaism—comes pouring in.

When Rilke says that he wants to unfold, that he doesn't "want to stay folded anywhere," in comes the Shekinah. When Pablo Neruda announces that now he will count to twelve "and you keep quiet and I will go," he invites us into the holy silence where the Shekinah dwells. Mary Oliver welcomes the Shekinah with her wish to be able to say, when it's all over, "all my life I was a bride married to amazement." And in her Passover poem Lyn Unger identifies the Shekinah as "that fierce presence" and reminds us that God never promised that we'd make it out of this world alive, but that rather "we might, at last, glimpse the stars, brilliant in the desert sky."

I find all this talk of burning and dissolving a deep comfort. Pema Chodron has spent the past half century recapitulating the teachings of the Buddha, steering us away from false expectations that the ache of the human experience is going to be magically resolved by divine intervention, and that our reward for the rigorous discipline of the spiritual path will be elite access to the instructor's edition of the Book of Life—in which the multiple-choice answers are written in black and white and all we need to do is fill in the blanks. Unknowingness is in itself sacred. This is the lifeblood of the poet-mystics.

"The important thing," said the Spanish mystic Teresa of Avila, "is not to think much, but to love much, and so to do whatever best awakens you to love." Not that there is anything inherently wrong with thinking. It might be tempting to reduce the power of poetry to mere irrationality, and in doing so miss the many treasures available through intellectual rigor. Mystical poetry does not bypass the rational mind. The bones of a good poem are built in the workshop of the mind, drawing on materials gathered with care, utilizing the tools of deep study and robust spiritual practice, dipped in the liquid gold of love-longing.

Nor is mystical poetry entirely iconoclastic. Most of the great masters whose words we love and quote spent their lives immersed in their own religious traditions, deeply devoted to the revelations at their core, even (perhaps especially) when they were busy trying to reform them. The nourishment offered by mystical poetry is cultivated in the garden of wisdom. The intoxicating power of a good poem begins with intention, strengthened by attention, and only then may be transmuted into a substance that changes the way we see and experience reality.

And so it is with awakening.

First we clothe ourselves in lucid contemplation and precise language. Then we get to peel it all off so that we can have a naked encounter with the beloved. The poet speaks to herself. "Dance, Lalla, with nothing on but the air," writes the fourteenth-century Kashmiri poet. "Sing, Lalla, wearing the sky."

After decades of spiritual inquiry, grounded in scholarship and reinvigorated by contemplative practice, I have not found a more ample threshold for entering the mystical consciousness than a poem. A succulent, awe-drenched, earth-bound, sublimely ordinary poem.

The Human Journey

SHAKTI CATERINA MAGGI

Consciousness has been radiating itself since the beginning of time. All forms we see are rays of this one eternal sunshine. Each ray is one with its source, made out of the same substance. As those rays travel through time and space, meeting matter and creating it, appearing as it, this eternal sun experiences change. Although this sun is unchangeable, it experiences change as the illusion of time and space. Out of its indivisible and neutral nature, consciousness experiences duality, polarities—learns and dissolves them in itself once again.

The incredible human journey is not made by a human being, but by your transcendental being. You are not a human being looking for God, but a spiritual being living a human experience. As a form, as this ray of light, you are an emanation of the divine, its expression. Your deepest nature does not belong to form. Every form belongs to you.

The incredible human journey is therefore about meeting matter and expressing it as form. Nothingness expresses itself consciously as everything, as a vibration of its own being. Every aspect of you as a form is simply a vibration of nothingness. In yourself, you remain still, silent, peaceful. You are not destroyable and you were never born. You cannot die. As Shankaracharya said: "I am Shiva, I am Shiva, I am Shiva." None of the qualities of the body can describe me. No seed of father made me.

You don't come from matter; matter comes from you. Form is a vibration of your true nature. When form is no longer coming through the impression of separation, it is not filtered by it and expresses your true being directly. As attention returns to you as silence, all those false impressions are dissolved. This happens through the heart, the bridge between form and emptiness, the sublime door between spiritual and material. The heart is emptiness consciously contemplating manifestation, the essence of being human, the exquisite jewel of the divine.

When consciousness is not aware of itself, the sense of separation will be projected onto the game of life as situations or people that represent this inner conflict. It is all impersonal, though it can be taken as very personal if there is no clarity that the world is you. These false impressions can reappear many times, before being seen as a reflection of an inner movement of consciousness. Once these conflicts are brought through your heart to the void of being, they will be reabsorbed in you as void. At that point the energy that is no longer engaged in manifesting mechanisms for protection of the imaginary person is available again to radiate *you*. So from *what* you really are—emptiness—you can express *who* you really are. This movement of individualization is part of the divine nature; although you are absolute transcendence, your expression is individualization. Though it remains one, the infinite expression of oneness manifests itself as many. Just like a rainbow, in its many vibrations of color, remains one light. We are this one light.

The illusion of "we" is the glorious emanation of oneness experiencing the vertigo of being human. That is why being here is the prize, the reward—being human, being alive in the human form. As this one consciousness meets and creates matter out of its own being, out of the same substance, the divine meets the form and its apparent limitations. This is a miracle. Something that knows no quality or limitation whatsoever can meet limitations. Often in our spiritual journey we get it completely wrong—as if we were a limited and separated entity who needs something more vast to be complete. With this wrong impression, the seeking goes on, looking for the next unfindable experience to complete us. Oneness cannot be found in a fragment; it can be found only in nothingness. Then, from the void, you can enjoy the manifestation as your glorious expression.

At that point, consciously, you will express your divine nature, unfiltered by the sense of separation. In coming back to the source, to the silence and true peace of your being, a new emanation, a new world can arise from your divine nature...and we all want it.

This is the desire of oneness: a new world not coming through the impression of separation, but through the return to the source, so that life—as the embodiment of the void—expresses you consciously. When all false impressions of separation are reabsorbed into oneness, something different appears spontaneously. From you, a new world will be projected.

It is actually happening now. It has always been happening. We are redeeming the world every moment. In one moment all this is here; then it collapses back into nothingness; then it reappears as this. You don't come and go in this appearance and disappearance, but the change is your direct expression. That is why it is so important that your life belongs to your heart and not to the self-image you construct.

This is not a mission for the apparent person. The making of a life that belongs to your heart is already happening. The life you experience is already a movement of this realization. What you call a spiritual crisis is life guiding you. Life is always teaching you the possibility of living from the heart, of living a life that belongs to your true self. For this to happen, false images of you have to be abandoned. Life, very lovingly, takes away whatever is no longer necessary. Life, as a movement of void, is the mother. It is Shakti dancing out of Shiva, guiding her children back home.

That is why attachments to false impressions need to be seen thoroughly. If you can remain open and perceive them—instead of avoiding them or trying to fix them or mend them—then the lesson is learned and that apparently lost fragment of you is brought back home to your heart.

ON THE MYSTERY OF BEING

This happens through the grace of God, not as the action of an apparent person. It is not homework. Consciousness itself learns about itself, awakens to itself. That is the prize of the divine, its ultimate glory. This human journey is therefore about heaven on earth. Heaven is not away from life; it is here, if you have eyes to see it. The invitation to heaven is in meeting life as it is, as *you*. It is a door to love and freedom at the same time: freedom from the illusion of being separated and love as an expression of you.

Receive what has been given to you every day as a gift from the divine, even when it is tough. Sometimes it is called "disease" or "grief" or "loss," sometimes falling in love or having a baby. Every day is different, but can you meet it as you? In this lies the beauty of living that can be truly seen if observed by your divine nature. Then transcendence and immanence will be the breath of the divine, and your form its precious vessel.

Even after awakening, life will test you, to meet everything as an expression of you—apparent enemies, difficulties, conflicts with your family, your government, everything. Being human is about becoming sensitive again: to see this illusion in all its rawness, its violent innocence, its tender wildness. That is its beauty and glory. If you can be this, then you are truly a Buddha!

Afterword:
On the Relationship Between Science and Liberation

MICHAEL A. SINGER

From the beginning of human time, humans have asked the question, what's going on out there? There are all these things: clouds, planets, rocks, animals—where did they come from? What is it? Plato asked. Aristotle asked. All of them asked.

We are fortunate to live in a time where we're finding out phenomenal answers to these questions. Newton didn't look at things the way Einstein did. In those days they saw a complete distinction between energy, the forces of nature, and matter. Einstein gave us a great gift. He followed form all the way down, past molecules and atoms, past electrons, neutrons, and protons. What a brilliant mind he had to see that behind it all it was just energy! This is just a dance of energy. In his words "Energy is matter and matter is energy, and the difference is just a temporary state."

We live in an age where quantum physics has found wavelets of underlying energy going through their cosmic dance of peaks and troughs, and throwing off subatomic particles. They throw off forces, tiny forces, that have characteristics and qualities—quarks, leptons, bosons. And these come together to interact in that space just outside the energy field and create the entire world we live in. That is an amazing thing to have figured out.

Even the fundamental forces of electromagnetism, strong and weak nuclear, and potentially gravity are just bosons popping out of these fields of energy interacting with the other particles to make up everything. The galaxies themselves are made of the quantum field. Interstellar space is made of the quantum field. Everything is the quantum field. There is nothing but that.

That's fascinating. But what does it have to do with the deep nondualist teachings that have been passed down for thousands of years in the Buddhist and yoga traditions?

What the great yogis found when they dropped into the source of their awareness is something that doesn't manifest from the quantum field but is actually the cause of it: consciousness. Consciousness is the most powerful underlying force in creation. All of creation manifests from consciousness. Consciousness manifests as form, and pure consciousness looks at that form. That's the truth of nonduality—it is all consciousness.

If that is the truth, why are we not living that truth? Why are we not in awe at the very fact that what we're looking at is the same energy manifesting in the diversity of form?

Because what has developed in the space between consciousness and manifestation is this thing called the psyche. Instead of understanding that everything's the same, we develop this psychological mumbo jumbo in our minds that says, "I matter. I am separate. I am different, and things should be the way I want."

That's the definition of ego. The absurdity of the individuality of self, of thinking that because your consciousness is limited by your senses, there's something special about what you see. There's nothing special about what happens to you. It has nothing to do with you. It has been going on for 13.8 billion years, everywhere.

What is true is that quantum energy, the quantum fields, consciousness, permeates the entire universe. It is omnipresent.

The highest spiritual technique is to actually live that truth. But we don't live like that. We come home and get frustrated. We yell at our loved ones. We get mad because our car has a scratch. We constantly live at a level that has nothing to do with what science has taught us. Science is challenging us to transcend the illusion of the appearance of things and to actually live the truth of what's going on, to bring harmony in this world, and to bring enlightenment within oneself.

We are here for a billionth of a trillionth of a second. We experience a billionth of a trillionth of it and believe we know what's going on. The truth is we have no idea what's going on. We just know that we exist. We are conscious, and we should be honored to be able to experience this phenomenal dance of manifestation.

If you do that, if you honor and respect and love all that is unfolding in creation, if you let go of that made-up individuality that has developed within the psyche, then there's nothing left but truth. Consciousness touching consciousness. That is the merger. That is what Christ meant when he said, "I and my father are one."

That is what all the great masters meant, those who released their sense of individuality, fell back into the seat of consciousness, and merged.

Science is a great thing. It is not against religion. It can actually be the essence and underlying force that leads us to God, if we are willing to live it. Not just study it, but live it every second of our lives. Our scientists are like our priests, our teachers. If we live what they teach us—the Oneness of all things—we need no other teachings.

Contributors

Adyashanti, author of *The Most Important Thing*, is a spiritual teacher devoted to serving the awakening of all beings. Asked to teach in 1996 by his Zen teacher of fourteen years, he invites students to stop and recognize what is true and liberating at the core of all existence. He lives in California with his wife, Mukti (also a spiritual teacher), and offers retreats, intensives, and Internet broadcasts.

adyashanti.org

Born in the Middle East, **A. H. Almaas** moved to the USA to study general relativity and nuclear physics at the University of California at Berkeley. A turning point in his life led him to inquire into the psychological and spiritual aspects of human nature. He founded the Diamond Approach—a teaching where the practice is the expression of realization, opening up the infinite creativity of our being. His books include *Runaway Realization*.

ahalmaas.com

Chameli Ardagh is the founder of Awakening Women, a women's wisdom school devoted to reclaiming a humanity rooted in the Mother. She is a passionate practitioner of embodied feminine spirituality and has, for more than two decades, inspired thousands of women around the world through embodied spiritual awakening practices. She is especially appreciated for her passionate love of mythology and storytelling as a method for awakening and embodiment.

awakeningwomen.com

Without diploma or culture, **Eric Baret** has no special competence. Touched by the nondual tradition, through Jean Klein's teaching, he proposes that one turns toward listening, free of any notion of gain. Nothing taught, no teacher. He holds meetings for the joy of being nothing.

bhairava.ws

Mauro Bergonzi taught Indian Religion and Philosophy at the University of Naples from 1985 to 2017. About twenty years ago—after twenty-five years of meditative practices—his spiritual seeking faded out, spontaneously and unexpectedly, and only a radical nondualism prevailed. From then, he has been invited to hold regular meetings of "sharing of being" *(satsang)*. A survey of Bergonzi's nondual communication is available in his book *Il sorriso segreto dell'essere*, and at:

sites.google.com/site/ilsorrisodellessere.

Michaela Boehm teaches and counsels internationally as an expert on intimacy and sexuality. In her work, she combines her psychology training and extensive clinical counseling experience with her in-depth training in the yogic arts as a classical Kashmiri Tantric lineage holder. She is the author of *The Wild Woman's Way*.

michaelaboehm.com

Cynthia Bourgeault is an Episcopal priest, internationally acclaimed writer and retreat leader, and a core faculty member at the Center for Action and Contemplation in Albuquerque, New Mexico. Her passion lies in bringing the Christian contemplative tradition into active dialogue with the other great nondual lineages of the world. She is the author of nine books, including *The Heart of Centering Prayer*, as well as many articles.

cynthiabourgeault.org

Fritjof Capra, PhD, physicist and systems theorist, is the author of several international bestsellers, including *The Tao of Physics* (1975). He is coauthor, with Pier Luigi Luisi, of the multidisciplinary textbook *The Systems View of Life* (Cambridge University Press, 2014). Capra's online course, capracourse.net, is based on this textbook.

fritjofcapra.net

Jude Currivan is a cosmologist, planetary healer, futurist, author, and, previously, a senior international businesswoman. She has an Oxford University MA in physics, specializing in cosmology, and a PhD in researching ancient cosmologies. She has worked with wisdom keepers in eighty countries, and researches the nature of reality. Author of six books, most recently *The Cosmic Hologram*, she is cofounder of WholeWorld-View and a member of the Evolutionary Leaders circle.

judecurrivan.com

Scientist **Bruce Damer** codeveloped the Hot Spring Hypothesis for the origin of life at University of California, Santa Cruz, and works with NASA and the space community in developing an architecture enabling the expansion of life and humanity into the cosmos.

damer.com

Zhen Dao is the founder of Post-Daoism and the MogaDao Institute. MogaDao encompasses five disciplines that are original in scope, movement, and philosophy—qigong, yoga, empty sky meditation, depth sexology, and psychospiritual martial arts—as well as the Heartmind Warrior Training and the Erotic Basis of Being programs. Zhen Dao, a transgender woman, is also a poet, novelist, playwright, and founder and director of the SACRA Theater Company.

mogadaoinstitute.com

Vera de Chalambert is a spiritual storyteller and Harvard-educated scholar of comparative religion. She speaks and writes about spiritual culture, mindfulness, and the emergence of feminine wisdom in our times. Her work explores the meeting place of theology, spirituality, and social change, and is informed by interspiritual insights from the world's great wisdom traditions. She holds a master's degree from Harvard Divinity School.

healingawakening.com

Larry Dossey is an internal medicine physician, former chief of staff of Medical City Dallas Hospital, and former co-chairman of the Panel on Mind/Body Interventions at the National Center for Complementary and Alternative Medicine. He is executive editor of the journal *Explore: The Journal of Science and Healing* and author of thirteen books on the role of consciousness and spirituality in health, the most recent being *One Mind*. Dossey lectures around the world.

dosseydossey.com

Charles Eisenstein is the author of *Climate: A New Story* and other books.

charleseisenstein.org

Ellen Emmet offers meetings and retreats in which the body and the felt experience are explored from a nondual perspective. She is a somatic psychotherapist and Authentic Movement practitioner, based in the UK. Her work with clients and groups is informed by her deep understanding of our shared essential reality.

ellenemmet.com

James Fadiman, PhD, has been a professor, a management consultant, a teacher of seminars worldwide, and has been involved in psychedelic research since the 1960s. One of the founders of Transpersonal Psychology, he is currently exploring the effects of microdoses on a variety of conditions, and has just completed a book, *Healthy Multiplicity* (with Jordan Gruber), on the selves within us.

jamesfadiman.com

Chris Fields explores the consequences of treating all interactions as observations, and hence regarding the world as composed entirely of observers observing each other. He is interested in how observers draw boundaries around parts of their experiences to separate out "entities," including themselves.

chrisfieldsresearch.com

Jeff Foster studied astrophysics at Cambridge University. In his twenties, after a period of depression and illness, he became addicted to the idea of "spiritual enlightenment" and embarked on a quest for the ultimate truth. This spiritual search came crashing down with his recognition of the nondual nature of everything, and his discovery of the extraordinary in the ordinary. His latest book, *The Way of Rest*, is published by Sounds True.

lifewithoutacentre.com

Edward Frenkel is a professor of mathematics at University of California, Berkeley, member of the American Academy of Arts and Sciences, and winner of the Hermann Weyl Prize in mathematical physics. His latest book, *Love and Math*, was a *New York Times* bestseller and won the Euler Book Prize. It has been published in eighteen languages.

edwardfrenkel.com

Gangaji travels the world speaking to spiritual seekers from all walks of life. A teacher and author, she powerfully articulates how it is possible to directly experience the truth of who you are and, in doing so, to discover true peace and lasting fulfillment. She lives with her husband in Oregon and is the author of *The Diamond in Your Pocket*.

gangaji.org

Stuart Hameroff, MD, is an anesthesiologist and professor at the University of Arizona, studying how the brain produces consciousness. Focusing on quantum vibrations of microtubules inside brain neurons, he teams with physicist Sir Roger Penrose on the controversial "Orch OR" theory, linking consciousness to the fine-scale structure of the universe. He directs clinical research on brain ultrasound to treat mental and cognitive disorders, and runs the Science of Consciousness conference series.

consciousness.arizona.edu

Kabir Helminski is a translator of the works of Rumi and others, a Shaikh of the Mevlevi Order, co-director of the Threshold Society, and a director of the Baraka Institute. His books have been published in at least eight languages. Among his most recent publications is *The Book of Language*. In 2009 he was named one of the five hundred most influential Muslims in the world.

sufism.org

Donald Hoffman is a professor of cognitive sciences at the University of California, Irvine. He received a PhD from MIT and the Troland Research Award from the US National Academy of Sciences. His work has been featured in *Wired*, *Quanta*, *The Atlantic*, *Discover Magazine*, and *Scientific American*. He has a book titled *The Case Against Reality* and a TED talk titled "Do We See Reality as It Is?"

socsci.uci.edu/~ddhoff/

Jean Houston, PhD, scholar and philosopher, is one of the foremost visionary thinkers of our time. She is regarded as one of the founders of the Human Potential Movement and is noted for her ability to combine her knowledge of history, culture, science, and spirituality into her teaching. She is chancellor of Meridian University and author of more than thirty books, the most recent being *What Is Consciousness?*, co-authored with Ervin Laszlo and Larry Dossey.

jeanhouston.com

Dorothy Hunt serves as spiritual director of Moon Mountain Sangha, teaching in the spiritual lineage of Adyashanti, who invited her to share the dharma in 2004. She has practiced psychotherapy since 1967 and is the founder of the San Francisco Center for Meditation and Psychotherapy. Her most recent publication is *Ending the Search*.

dorothyhunt.org

Most recently the author of *The Idea of the World*, **Bernardo Kastrup** has a PhD in computer engineering, with specializations in artificial intelligence and reconfigurable computing. He has worked as a scientist in some of the world's foremost research laboratories and has authored many academic papers on science and philosophy.

bernardokastrup.com

Sally Kempton is a spiritual teacher who offers workshops and retreats, both online and in person. She is the author of *Meditation for the Love of It*.

sallykempton.com

Stephen LaBerge, PhD, pioneer in the scientific study of lucid dreaming, received his degree in psychophysiology from Stanford University. In 1987, he founded the Lucidity Institute, to research the nature and potential of human consciousness for the enhancement of health and well-being. His current research includes studies on the psychophysiological correlates of various states of consciousness. Published works include *Exploring the World of Lucid Dreaming*.

lucidity.com

Robert Lanza, MD, is author of *Biocentrism* and *Beyond Biocentrism*. He is currently head of Astellas Global Regenerative Medicine, chief scientific officer of AIRM, and a professor at Wake Forest University. *Time* magazine recognized him as one of the "100 Most Influential People in the World," and *Prospect* magazine named him one of the Top 50 "World Thinkers."

robertlanza.com

Peter A. Levine, PhD, holds doctorates in both biophysics and psychology. He is the developer of Somatic Experiencing®, a naturalistic and neurobiological approach to healing trauma. He is founder of the Somatic Experiencing® Trauma Institute/Foundation for Human Enrichment®, founder and president of Ergos Levine Institute of Somatic Education®, and author of several best-selling books on trauma, including *Waking the Tiger*, which has been published in close to thirty languages.

somaticexperiencing.com

Lynn Marie Lumiere, MFT, is a nondual psychotherapist and author with a focus on transforming issues at their source, through dissolving the belief in separation that creates and sustains them. She is a repeat presenter at the Conference on Nondual Wisdom and Psychotherapy and the Science and Nonduality Conference, and she is the author of *Awakened Relating.*

lynnmarielumiere.com

Shakti Caterina Maggi has been sharing a message of awakening to our true nature as One Consciousness since 2003, with workshops and meetings held around the world. She shares a contemporary approach to self-realization and reveals the real possibility of seeing what we are and embodying it in our everyday life with clarity, wisdom, and humor.

shakticaterinamaggi.com

Gabor Maté, a retired physician, is an internationally published author of four books, translated into twenty-five languages, including the award-winning bestseller *In the Realm of Hungry Ghosts*. A public speaker in great demand, he is now working on his next book, *The Myth of Normal.*

drgabormate.com

Dean Radin, PhD, is chief scientist at the Institute of Noetic Sciences and a professor at the California Institute of Integral Studies. He is author or coauthor of hundreds of technical and magazine articles, including a hundred peer-reviewed articles in professional journals, four dozen book chapters, and four popular books, including *Real Magic*.

deanradin.org

Peter Russell is a leading thinker on consciousness and contemporary spirituality, and the author of ten books, including *The Global Brain*. His mission is to distill the essential wisdom on human consciousness found in the world's various spiritual traditions, and to disseminate their teachings on self-liberation in contemporary and compelling ways.

peterrussell.com

Corine Sombrun grew up in Africa and studied musicology, piano, and composition in France. She settled in London in 1999 and undertook projects for the BBC World Service. One of these took her to Mongolia, where she was invited to undertake the training to become a shaman. After eight years, she became the first Western woman fully trained in the Mongolian shamanic tradition. Sombrun has written several books translated into many languages, including *In Geronimo's Footsteps*.

corinesombrun.com

From an early age, **Rupert Spira** was deeply interested in the nature of reality. In 1997 he met his teacher, Francis Lucille, who introduced him to the Direct Path teachings of Atmananda Krishnamenon, to Jean Klein, and to the tantric tradition of Kashmir Shaivism—and, more important, directly indicated to him the true nature of experience. Spira is author of several books, including *The Nature of Consciousness*.

rupertspira.com

Paul Stamets, speaker, author, mycologist, medical researcher, and entrepreneur, is an intellectual and industry leader in fungi. He lectures extensively, showing how mushrooms can help the health of people and planet. His passion is to preserve and protect ancestral strains of mushrooms. He is the author of six books, has discovered and named numerous new species of mushrooms, and is the founder and owner of Fungi Perfecti.

fungi.com

Henry Stapp received his PhD in particle physics at the University of California, Berkeley. He worked with Wolfgang Pauli and Werner Heisenberg on fundamental issues surrounding quantum mechanics. After returning to Berkeley he published an influential article, "The Copenhagen Interpretation," in the *American Journal of Physics*. Stapp has made major contributions to understanding the quantum connection of mind to physical processes. His latest book is *Quantum Theory and Free Will.*

Mirabai Starr writes creative nonfiction and contemporary translations of sacred literature. She taught Philosophy and World Religions at the University of New Mexico, Taos, for twenty years and now teaches and speaks internationally on contemplative practice and interspiritual dialogue. Her latest book is *Wild Mercy: Living the Fierce and Tender Wisdom of the Women Mystics.* She lives with her extended family in the mountains of northern New Mexico.

mirabaistarr.com

Neil D. Theise, MD, is Professor of Pathology at New York University School of Medicine. He is a pioneering researcher in adult stem cells, human liver cancer, and the identification of previously unrecognized anatomy of the human interstitium, which he contends warrants recognition as a "new organ." He is also a Jewish practitioner, a senior student at the Village Zendo in New York (with teacher Roshi Enkyo O'Hara), and a recent shamanic initiate.

neiltheise.com

Robert Thurman is Professor of Indo-Tibetan Buddhist Studies in the department of religion at Columbia University; president of the Tibet House U.S., a nonprofit dedicated to the preservation and promotion of Tibetan civilization; and president of the American Institute of Buddhist Studies, which publishes translations of important treatises from the Tibetan Tengyur. His latest book is *Man of Peace: The Illustrated Life Story of the Dalai Lama of Tibet.*

bobthurman.com

Joan Tollifson writes and talks about being awake to the aliveness and immediacy of what is. Her bare-bones approach is open, direct, and down-to-earth. She is the author of four books, including *Nothing to Grasp.* She is at work on a book about aging and dying, and lives in southern Oregon.

joantollifson.com

Pim van Lommel, MD, started his research on near-death experience (NDE) in 1986, and his study on NDE in survivors of cardiac arrest was published in *The Lancet* in 2001. His Dutch book *Eindeloos bewustzijn* was nominated for the 2008 Book of the Year in the Netherlands and has been translated into nine languages. The English translation, *Consciousness Beyond Life,* received the 2010 Book Award of the Scientific and Medical Network in the UK.

consciousnessbeyondlife.com

Unmani meets you in the midst of your unique personal experience, while at the same time holding you in your absolute nature. This combination of personal and impersonal brings deep rest and wholeness. Unmani is from England, but for fifteen years has been living and teaching in many countries. She is a mother and an ordinary woman. Unmani has published three books, the best-known being *Die to Love.*

die-to-love.com

Pamela Wilson travels widely in the United States, Canada, Europe, and Central America, holding *satsang* and giving private sessions and weeklong retreats, speaking the truth of nonduality. She has endeared herself to many through her lighthearted humor and compassion, and her deep understanding of what it is to be human. She lives in Northern California. Her latest book is *The Golden Retriever's Guide to Joy.*

pamelasatsang.com

Julie Brown Yau's three decades in psychological, somatic, and spiritual traditions provide a unique depth of knowledge and experience. Her psychological and spiritual practice embedded a deep passion for resolving trauma and cultivating compassion and joy in our lives. Julie is an author and speaker and is in private practice in Laguna Beach, California. Her latest book is *The Body Awareness Workbook for Trauma.*

juliebrownyau.com

Mauro Zappaterra, MD, PhD, graduated from Harvard Medical School and now specializes in physical medicine and rehabilitation. He is also trained in biodynamic craniosacral therapy, polarity therapy, and reiki. He is the medical director of various multidisciplinary pain rehabilitation programs integrating comprehensive, multimodality treatment plans, to help people fully realize their potential. He has published numerous scientific papers on the function of the cerebrospinal fluid.

holdingspace.com

Zaya Benazzo is a filmmaker from Bulgaria with degrees in engineering, environmental science, and film. For many years, she worked as an environmental activist in Holland and Bulgaria, and later produced and directed several award-winning documentaries in Europe and the United States.

Maurizio Benazzo grew up in Italy, and in 1984 came to the United States on a ninety-eight-year-old sailing boat. He started working as an actor, model, and filmmaker, but his thirst for knowledge was only satisfied in 2001 upon encountering *I Am That*, the seminal work by Sri Nisargadatta Maharaj, while he was in India shooting the award-winning documentary *Short Cut to Nirvana*.

Maurizio and Zaya merged their lifelong passions for science and mysticism when they met in 2007, and their first project together was filming the documentary *Rays of the Absolute* on the life and teachings of Sri Nisargadatta Maharaj. This project sparked their next level of creation and collaboration: Science and Nonduality (SAND)—a global community inspired by the timeless wisdom traditions, informed by modern science, and grounded in direct experience.

Foreword writer **Deepak Chopra** is author of more than seventy books, including numerous *New York Times* bestsellers. His medical training is in internal medicine and endocrinology.

Afterword writer **Michael A. Singer** is author of the *New York Times* bestseller, *The Untethered Soul*, which has also been published in numerous languages around the world.

Register your **new harbinger** titles for additional benefits!

When you register your **new harbinger** title—purchased in any format, from any source—you get access to benefits like the following:

- Downloadable accessories like printable worksheets and extra content

- Instructional videos and audio files

- Information about updates, corrections, and new editions

Not every title has accessories, but we're adding new material all the time.

Access free accessories in 3 easy steps:

1. Sign in at NewHarbinger.com (or **register** to create an account).

2. Click on **register a book**. Search for your title and click the **register** button when it appears.

3. Click on the **book cover or title** to go to its details page. Click on **accessories** to view and access files.

That's all there is to it!

If you need help, visit:

NewHarbinger.com/accessories

new harbinger
CELEBRATING
40 YEARS